PAGAN TRINITY

—

HOLY TRINITY

The Legacy of the Sumerians in Western Civilization

Alan Dickin

Hamilton Books
A member of
The Rowman & Littlefield Publishing Group
Lanham · Boulder · New York · Toronto · Plymouth, UK

Copyright © 2007 by
Hamilton Books
4501 Forbes Boulevard
Suite 200
Lanham, Maryland 20706
Hamilton Books Acquisitions Department (301) 459-3366

Estover Road
Plymouth PL6 7PY
United Kingdom

Library of Congress Control Number: 2007926688
ISBN-13: 978-0-7618-3777-0 (paperback : alk. paper)
ISBN-10: 0-7618-3777-9 (paperback : alk. paper)

Dedication

To the descendants of the Sumerians:
That they might rediscover their spiritual birthright

CONTENTS

PREFACE

Every year, another crop of first-year university students chooses Mythology 101 as one of their elective courses. What are they looking for, apart from an easy credit? Perhaps they're looking for the same thing that Mankind has been searching for since the dawn of History: the meaning of Life itself! If any people could speak with authority on this subject, surely it was the ancient Sumerians, whose mythology tells poignantly of the gaining and losing of Eternal Life and of Mankind's first experience of God. The religion of the Sumerians was itself lost to the world until a century ago, and having been found, presents a Gordian Knot of interwoven threads. However, this author is impetuous enough to cut the knot using the sharpest sword: the belief that the True God was indeed revealed in the world's oldest civilization . . . ancient Sumer.

ACKNOWLEDGEMENTS

All scripture references in this book are taken from the New International Version of the Bible, copyright by the New York International Bible Society. The author also acknowledges translations of other ancient sources by several scholars, who are cited at the end of each excerpt. Details of these publications are given in the bibliography.

All figures in this book were drawn by the author. However some of these were based on information from previously published sources, which are acknowledged in the figure captions where appropriate. Publication details are again given in the bibliography.

Finally, the author acknowledges Morning Star publications for the use of an original excerpt from *The Final Quest* by Rick Joyner (www.morningstarministries.org).

Chapter 1

Who were the Sumerians?

'Looters destroy Iraq's historical treasures'

So ran newspaper headlines in April 2003, when an orgy of destruction and looting followed the American conquest of Iraq (Figure 1.1). In the chaotic aftermath of war, the Iraq Museum and National Library in Baghdad were abandoned to their fate at the hands of roving mobs. The cultural desecration that followed was likened by many to the sack of Baghdad by the Mongols in 1258 AD, a wave of destruction that set Middle Eastern civilization back five hundred years . . .

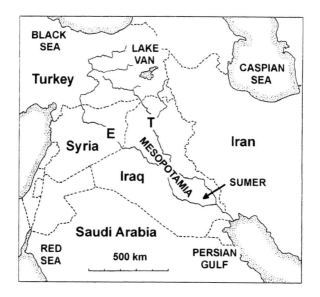

Figure 1.1. Map of the Middle East showing the land of Sumer situated between the Tigris and Euphrates rivers (T and E) within the borders of modern Iraq.

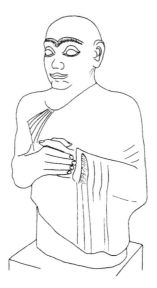

Figure 1.2. A statue of Gudea, ruler of Lagash around 2200 BC, which exudes an air of serene and confident spirituality. Diorite, British Museum.

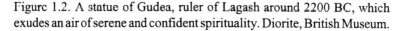

And yet the disaster of 2003 was the very thing that brought the civilization of ancient Iraq to world attention as never before. Newspapers ran stories about the art of ancient Mesopotamia and explained the meaning behind this name . . . Mesopotamia . . . the Greek words for the land between two great rivers, the Tigris and Euphrates (Figure 1.1). Some even mentioned the region in southern Mesopotamia that is widely believed to be the cradle of human civilization . . . ancient Sumer, and its inhabitants, the mysterious people we know as the Sumerians.

'Sumerian' was not the name that these ancient people gave to their own culture, but the name given to them by the Assyrian peoples of northern Mesopotamia. In their own language, the Sumerians called themselves *sag-gi-ga*, the 'dark-headed ones'. No-one knows the precise meaning of this expression, but the Sumerians are typically portrayed in their own art as having a rounded shaven head, prominent eyes, and clean-shaven chin. Their appearance is exemplified by Gudea, ruler of the city state of Lagash around 2200 BC, whose elegant diorite statues are displayed in the Musée du Louvre and the British Museum (Figure 1.2).

The Sumerians have rarely attracted the attention that they deserve in the history of civilization. In fact, the Sumerians practically *invented* civilization, a word which comes from the Latin *civis* (citizen) and actually means 'life in cities'. Before the appearance of the Sumerians, ancient peoples had been living in settlements and villages for centuries, ever since the 'agricultural revolution' around 7000 BC. However, the Sumerians built the world's first true cities in southern Mesopotamia, beginning around 5000 BC at Eridu and reaching a climax two thousand years later at Uruk.

Uruk is one of the first cities mentioned in the Bible (Genesis 10:10), where it is referred to in Hebrew as *Erech*. The city was inhabited for over four thousand years, and did not finally fall into decay until the third century AD. Today the site is known as Warka, and the ruined walls of the ancient city can still be traced in the desert of southern Iraq. Reaching up to fifty feet high, and with a length of over 6 miles (10 km), these walls enclose an area of over 550 hectares (5.5 square km). The archaeologist Hans Nissen highlighted the immense size of Uruk at the dawn of history by comparing an outline city plan of Uruk with other ancient cities (Figure 1. 3). The walls of Uruk enclose an area twice as large as Athens at the height of its power, and more than half the size of imperial Rome. Earlier prehistoric settlements such as Catal Huyuk and Jericho were tiny in comparison.

The achievements of the Sumerians are all the more remarkable when one considers that the land of Sumer had few natural resources . . . essentially no wood, stone or metals, or even any rain. In fact the only resource available to the Sumerians was the rich alluvial soil of the Mesopotamian plain, deposited over millennia by the flooding of its two great rivers. Because of the lack of rainfall in southern Mesopotamia, this land could only be cultivated by diverting river water through a complex system of canals to irrigate the fields. However, the organizational challenge of building this irrigation system provided the impetus for the development of complex social structures. Based on this achievement, the Sumerians were able to establish a thriving agricultural economy to support the earliest development of life in cities.

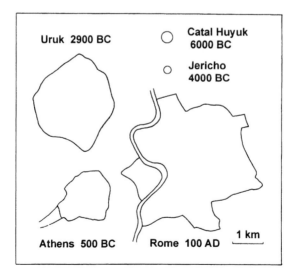

Figure 1.3. Plans showing the city walls of Uruk, Athens and Rome, compared with the estimated size of major prehistoric settlements, all to the same scale. City maps based on Nissen (1983).

Despite the success of their civilization, the Sumerians remain a people of mystery. Their language, reconstructed by 'Sumerologists', is unrelated to any other known language. They appear in the archaeological record out of nowhere, sometime around 5000 BC, and fade away again three thousand years later, swamped by waves of Semitic immigration to the plains of Mesopotamia. But despite their enigmatic story, the Sumerians gave the world some of its greatest inventions and cultural institutions, and gave us a record of their achievements by the tool that they themselves developed . . . the art of writing.

Samuel Noah Kramer, one of the great Sumerologists of the twentieth century, summarized some of their most notable achievements in his best-selling book 'History begins at Sumer' . . . the first schools, the first law codes, the first love poetry, the first epic literature, the first libraries . . . and many other firsts. But all of these great achievements by the Sumerians were merely off-shoots from a development that drove their whole way of life and which represents their most important contribution to human civilization . . . the first organized religion.

Today, religion has almost become a dirty word, bringing to mind systems of dogma and doctrine, but the original meaning of religion (Latin *religio*) was much more experiential. The worshipper sensed a power outside himself, and had a feeling of reverence towards that power which led to worship. These experiences

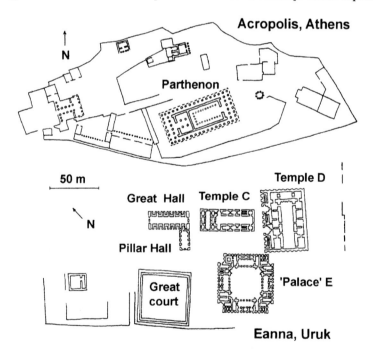

Figure 1.4. Comparison of the Eanna Complex of Uruk (ca. 3300 BC) with the Acropolis of Athens (ca. 500 BC), shown to the same scale.

of divine power and of the desire to worship found their sharpest focus in the institution of the temple, which was first developed by the Sumerians, and which formed the cornerstone of their civilization. And here again, the city of Uruk was pre-eminent.

At its zenith around 3000 BC, the city of Uruk boasted the greatest temple complex of the ancient world. Described by one scholar as a veritable 'cathedral city', this Eanna Complex was built on a man-made platform equivalent in area to the Athenian acropolis (Figure 1.4). As shown in this figure, the Eanna Complex was laid out with a monumental scale of architecture, consisting of great open spaces and massive buildings. These included a huge square structure sometimes called a palace (E), and an immense temple (D) that was 200 feet long and 130 feet wide (60 x 40 m). With its grandiose long nave and many ancillary rooms, this temple was comparable in size with the Parthenon, built nearly 3000 years later. Together, these buildings speak eloquently of the dominant focus of Sumerian civilization, the worship and service of the divine power of the gods.

Chapter 2

The discovery of ancient Sumer

In the seventeenth and eighteenth centuries, European travellers and adventurers began for the first time to penetrate the veil of secrecy that hung over the Middle East. From within the decaying empire of the Ottoman Turks, they brought back tales of lavish wealth and amazing monuments and ruins.

The land of Mesopotamia held a special fascination for Europeans, because of its description in the first chapters of the Bible as the cradle of human civilization. However, most travellers were appalled by the scene of desolation that presented itself, within the very land that had once been the Garden of Eden. William Loftus, first excavator of the city of Uruk, commented poignantly: 'Of all the desolate sights I ever beheld, that of Uruk incomparably surpasses all'.

Nevertheless, these ruins also instilled a sense of awe in the traveller, as we can see from J. P. Newman's description of the ruins of Birs Nimrud, once thought to be the original Tower of Babel (Figure 2.1):

> Rising suddenly out of the desert plain, a riven, fragmentary blasted pile . . . Such was the enchanting power of the vision that the eye was transfixed and the spell of history was upon the soul. Before us was the oldest historic monument known to man.

Figure 2.1. View of Birs Nimrud, near Babylon, based on an engraving by Newman (1876).

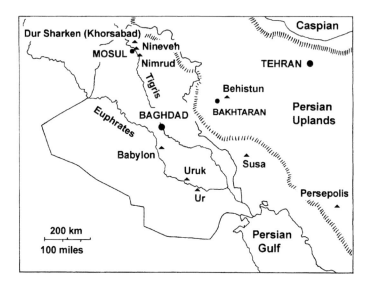

Figure 2.2. Map of Mesopotamia and western Persia (modern Iran), showing the locations of important ancient sites (▲) relative to modern cities (●). Fringes mark the edge of the Persian mountains.

The dawn of archaeological interest in Mesopotamia really began during the Napoleonic wars, when the British diplomat Claudius Rich was posted to an official Residency in Baghdad in order to safeguard British trading interests in the region. Rich became interested in the remains of ancient cities scattered around Baghdad (Figure 2.2), and in 1811 visited the ruins of Babylon. Rich made the first detailed survey of this site and published a memoir that aroused considerable interest in Mesopotamian archaeology back in England. In 1821, Rich died in a cholera epidemic at the age of only 34. However, his collection of Mesopotamian artifacts reached the British Museum four years after his death and became the foundation of its Western Asiatic (Middle Eastern) collection.

The British Residency in Baghdad was soon matched by the French, and their diplomat Paul-Emile Botta was the first European to begin major excavations in Mesopotamia. After some early failures, he achieved spectacular success when he began to dig at the mound of Khorsabad, 15 miles north of the city of Mosul in northern Iraq (Figure 2.2). Here, in 1843, he discovered an Assyrian royal palace with intricately-carved bas-relief wall sculptures that are now displayed in the Musée du Louvre in Paris. The palace is now known to be that of Sargon II (721-705 BC), after whom the city itself was named (*Dur Sharken*, or City of Sargon).

Inspired by Botta's success, the Englishman Austin Henry Layard began excavating in November 1845 at the mound of Nimrud, located 20 miles southeast of Mosul. In the beginning, Layard had no permission from the Ottoman Government to dig, no funding from the British Government, and not even an official job. However, his enthusiasm for ancient civilizations attracted the support of Sir Stratford Canning, British Ambassador to the Ottoman Empire in Constantinople. Canning paid for Layard's early excavations out of his own pocket, and thus secured for the British Museum one of the world's finest collections of Middle Eastern antiquities.

The mound of Nimrud, typical of many 'tells' in ancient Mesopotamia, consisted of a barren raised platform about 40 feet high, with a small pyramidal-shaped hill at the north end that represented the remains of an ancient ziggurat. Layard's method of excavation was to search for any signs of carved stone slabs around the edges of the mound, and then to follow these slabs into the centre of the mound by digging deep trenches along the old walls (Figure 2.3). By this means, Layard uncovered not one, but two Assyrian royal palaces in different parts of the mound, each with walls decorated in bas-relief and containing monumental stone sculptures.

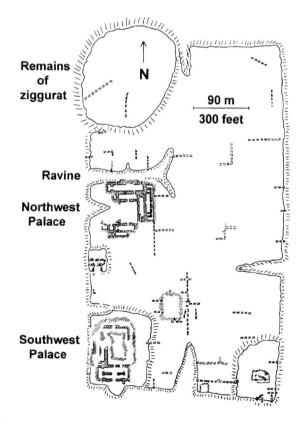

Figure 2.3. Layard's plan of the mound of Nimrud, showing his exploratory trenches (dashed lines), and the two major palaces that he unearthed. Heavy lines = carved stone wall facings. After Layard (1849).

The exposed stones around the edges of the mound had suffered considerable damage from the weather, so Layard decided to make use of a natural ravine that cut into the west side of the mound. By trenching into the walls of the ravine, Layard almost immediately struck carved stone walls that were in an excellent state of preservation. This was eventually revealed as the north-west palace of Nimrud.

The day after the discovery of the north-west palace, Layard went to visit one of the local Arab sheiks to pay a social call. By observing such rules of etiquette, Layard was able to maintain excellent relations with the local tribes; of vital necessity, since at that time he had no official permission from the Ottoman Government to dig. On his way back to the mound, he was met by two of his workmen in a state of great agitation. They had uncovered a giant human head in the bottom of the trench, which they believed to be none other than the hero Nimrod, famed in the Bible as the builder of the world's first cities (Gen 10:9). This head appeared to be ascending like an infernal object from the nether regions (Figure 2.4), and one of the terrified Arabs had immediately rushed back to the city of Mosul, announcing in the markets and bazaars that Nimrod himself had risen from the grave. The whole city was thrown into such an uproar that Layard was forced to close the excavations for several days until the hubbub had died down.

Figure 2.4. The discovery of the gigantic head at Nimrud, which was taken by the Arabs to be the resurrection of the biblical hero, Nimrod (Gen 10:9). Based on an engraving by Layard (1849).

Despite many other interruptions, Layard continued digging, and the news of his spectacular discoveries finally reached England. As a result of widespread public interest, Sir Stratford Canning was able to obtain a measure of public support from the British Government. This allowed him to obtain an official excavation permit or '*firman*' from the Ottoman Government and a small grant from the British Museum. This was forwarded to Layard with the stern injunction: "Obtain the greatest possible number of well-preserved objects of art at the least possible outlay of time and money."

Unfortunately, this kind of attitude was typical of those times, but Layard did the best he could in the circumstances, making many detailed drawings of objects too fragile to move. By the summer of 1847 he had excavated and crated many of the best wall reliefs, along with a monumental winged bull which turned out to be the owner of Nimrod's head. After much strenuous work, the ten-ton giant was loaded onto a pallet and sent down river by raft, along with a winged lion of similar size. Eventually they were shipped to London and exhibited in the British Museum (Figure 2.5), where they created a huge public sensation. In the meantime, Layard's book detailing his exploits was published under the title '*Nineveh and its Remains*'. Notwithstanding its somewhat misleading title, the book struck a chord with the public and became an instant best-seller.

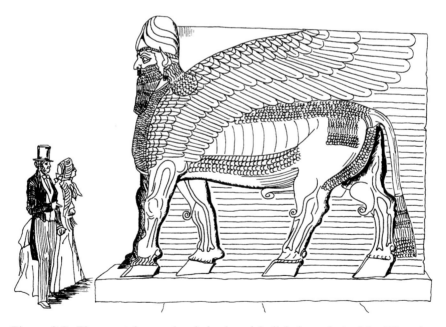

Figure 2.5. The great human-headed winged bull being admired by Victorian society in the British Museum. Based on an engraving from the *Illustrated London News* of October, 1850.

One of the most important discoveries at Nimrud, from an archaeological point of view, was a black stone obelisk, seven feet high, that was found in a wonderful state of preservation by Layard's workmen. The obelisk was carved in bas relief on all four sides, with several panels showing the King of Assyria receiving tribute from his vassals and subject peoples (e.g. Figure 2.6). When the inscription was later deciphered, it was found to commemorate the conquests of Shalmaneser III, King of Assyria in the middle of the 9th century BC. Of particular interest, however, was the inscription describing the panel in Figure 2.6:

> The tribute of Jehu, son of Omri: I received from him silver, gold, a golden bowl, a golden vase with painted bottom, golden tumblers, golden buckets, tin, a staff for a king, and fruits.
>
> [Translation: Barnett, 1966]

This text refers to King Jehu of Samaria, whose rise to power is described in the Old Testament book of Second Kings, Chapter 9. He became the ruler of the northern kingdom of Israel after killing King Joram (son of Ahab and grandson of Omri) in a *coup*. In the light of this background information, we can see that the phrase *Jehu, son of Omri* used on the obelisk was only an 'approximation' to the truth. However, it was consistent with the common practice of usurpers to style themselves as the true descendants of one of the earlier great kings of a royal lineage. As such, the obelisk of Shalmaneser was the first contemporary inscription to verify a piece of Old Testament history. It caused a great sensation, and led to the expectation that additional inscriptions from Mesopotamia would verify other stories of the Old Testament.

Figure 2.6. A scene from the obelisk of Shalmaneser III, showing Jehu, King of Israel (kneeling), presenting tribute to the King of Assyria. British Museum.

In 1849, Layard set out on his second expedition to Mesopotamia, and now began to excavate the much larger mound of Kuy-un-jik, just across the river from Mosul. Botta had excavated there in the early days, but had not dug deep enough into the mound to make significant finds. At Kuy-un-jik, Layard discovered the remains of Nineveh itself, including a huge royal palace decorated with many beautiful wall reliefs. In addition, he found the first fragments of the great library of the Assyrian king Ashur-banipal, dating from the 7th century BC. This library consisted of thousands of clay tablets which the king had collected from all over his empire, and would later be shown to contain such major literary works as the Mesopotamian version of the Flood Story.

While these ground-breaking discoveries were being made in the ruins of Mesopotamia, other European scholar-adventurers were studying inscriptions in western Persia (modern Iran). The earliest discoveries were made in the eighteenth century by two Danes, Carsten Niebuhr and Friedrich Munter, who studied monumental inscriptions at the ancient Persian capital of Persepolis (Figure 2.2). These inscriptions were all written in the wedge-shaped writing that came to be called 'cuneiform'. However, Niebuhr and Munter recognized from the variety of signs in some inscriptions that they were written in three different languages. One language used only 36 signs and therefore appeared to be alphabetic; the second used more than a hundred, and was therefore probably syllabic (as in Japanese); the third had nearly 600 signs, suggesting that it was a 'logographic' script, in which every word may have a different sign (as in Chinese). Examples of the three types of script are shown in Figure 2.7 for comparison.

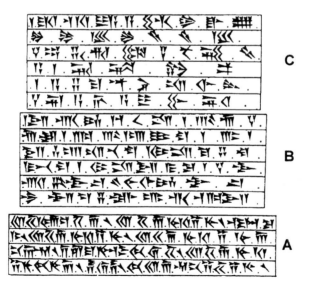

Figure 2.7. Cuneiform inscriptions from Persepolis in three ancient languages, believed to be: a) alphabetic; b) syllabic and c) logographic.

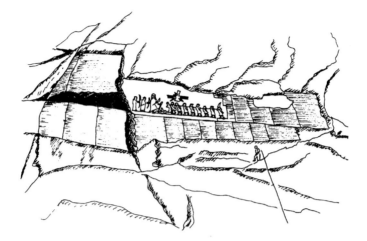

Figure 2.8. A view of the monumental inscription of Behistun, which commemorates the Persian king Darius, and is carved into a rock face 300 feet above the road from Tehran to Bakhtaran.

Munter suggested that the alphabetic script at Persepolis might be Old Persian, a language whose pronunciation was already partially understood, and soon afterwards this theory was confirmed by a German scholar, Georg Friedrich Grotefend. In 1802, Grotefend made the first breakthrough in the translation of cuneiform when he recognized the names of some of the most famous kings of the Persian Empire, Darius the Great and his son Xerxes. The remaining stages in the decipherment of the cuneiform script were made principally by three rival scholars, Henry Creswicke Rawlinson, Edward Hincks and Jules Oppert, sometimes referred to as the 'holy triad of cuneiform studies.'

Rawlinson was an officer in the (British) Indian Army who was posted as military advisor to the Persian government in 1835. He was also a keen linguist, and continued the work of Grotefend using several monumental inscriptions. Rawlinson's main contribution to the decipherment of Persian cuneiform came from his work on the great trilingual inscription at Behistun (also called Bisitun), located 20 miles east of Bakhtaran in the Zagros Mountains (Figure 2.2). This massive inscription, more than 60 feet wide and 20 feet high, is carved into a vertical cliff face 300 feet above the road (Figure 2.8). In the centre of the inscription, a bas-relief sculpture shows Darius the Great trampling one of his enemies underfoot and standing in judgement on nine rebel kings, chained together at the neck. Around this carved relief, the text of the inscription is written in the same three types of script previously seen at Persepolis. However, because of the great length of the Behistun text, it provided a much better chance of decipherment. Hence, this inscription proved to be the cuneiform equivalent of the 'Rosetta Stone', which had earlier allowed the decipherment of Egyptian hieroglyphics.

The Behistun inscription was known to Europeans before Rawlinson, but had never been copied in detail. Between 1835 and 1837, Rawlinson succeeded in copying most of the Old Persian script, which was located on the lower part of the monument, above a ledge in the cliff (Figure 2.9). The work was interrupted by a posting back to India, but Rawlinson was able to return a few years later when he became the representative of the British Government in Baghdad. He now brought ladders to reach the upper parts of the Persian text, but the narrowness of the ledge made the task unexpectedly difficult. To allow a reasonable inclination against the rock face, Rawlinson was forced to chop the top off his ladder, and then to stand on the topmost rung, spread-eagled against the sheer rock face as he copied the cuneiform signs into his notebook. Finally, by 1847, he had recovered the complete inscription in Old Persian and published its translation. It turned out not to be a truly alphabetic script, but one based largely on vowel-consonant pairs.

The second and third scripts at Behistun were much more complex. Rough copies could be made from a distance, but for detailed study it was necessary to obtain 'squeezes', by pressing *papier mâché* into the cuneiform indentations carved into the rock face. After it has dried, the *papier mâché* can be removed, and then bears an exact cast of the inscription. The second script was at the left end of the monument (Figure 2.9), where the ledge was interrupted for some distance by a sheer precipice. Rawlinson was forced to use ladders to bridge across the gap, and his first attempt, with his 'cut-off' short ladder was nearly fatal when the ladder gave way. Later, he obtained a longer ladder to bridge the gap, and then rested a short ladder on this 'bridge' to reach the inscription. Surely this was not work for the faint-hearted!

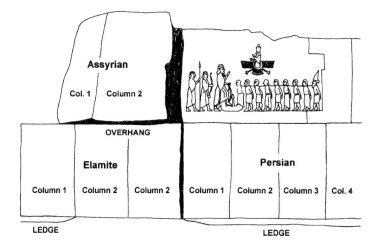

Figure 2.9. Detailed view of the trilingual inscription of Darius the Great at Behistun, showing the locations of the different texts on the rock face.

The second script at Behistun was eventually shown to be Elamite, the language of the people of SW Iran, whose capital was the ancient city of Susa. However, the third script was of greatest interest, since it matched the writing then being recovered on tablets and inscribed bricks from the ruins of northern Mesopotamia. This 'Assyrian' script was located on an even more inaccessible part of the Behistun rock, above a large overhang in the cliff (Figure 2.9). The problem seemed impossible until a Kurdish boy clawed his way across the sheer rock face with a rope, and then made squeezes of the vital inscription under Rawlinson's direction. This material allowed Rawlinson, Hincks and Oppert to decipher the so-called Assyrian Cuneiform script by 1857 and to recognize its pronunciation as part of the Semitic group of languages.

This script had barely been deciphered when Rawlinson discovered yet another kind of cuneiform writing on inscriptions from Southern Mesopotamian cities such as Uruk and Isin (Figure 2.10). This script was clearly different from any of the three types at Persepolis and Behistun. However, once the new script had been recognized, it was also found on 'bilingual' tablets from Nineveh, along with the newly deciphered 'Assyrian' writing. By studying how Semitic names were transliterated into this new script, it was possible to determine the pronunciation of the unknown language associated with the script. The results showed that the new script represented a completely new language that was not of Semitic type at all, but of unknown linguistic affinity.

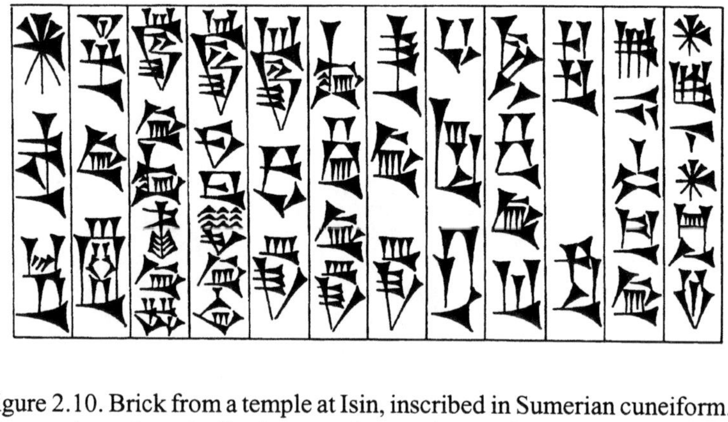

Figure 2.10. Brick from a temple at Isin, inscribed in Sumerian cuneiform. The text is read vertically downwards, starting on the right hand side. In the translation opposite, slashes indicate new columns. British Museum.

In 1861, Rawlinson presented the inscription in Figure 2.10, which was one of the earliest texts in this new language to be published and translated. It was inscribed on the bricks of a temple built around 2000 BC, and commemorates the piety of a king from the city state of Isin for his support of temples in the Mesopotamian cities of Nippur, Ur, Eridu and Uruk. However, most importantly, the tenth panel from the right refers to the two main political regions of Mesopotamia, *ki-engi* and *ki-uri*, which we know as Sumer and Akkad:

Ishme-Dagan / provider of Nippur / support / of Ur /
who daily stands for / Eridu / priest of Uruk / mighty king / king of Isin /
king of Sumer and Akkad / beloved "spouse"/ of Inanna

[Translation: Bottero, 1987]

Based on the evidence from this inscription, Oppert recognized Akkad as the kingdom of the northern Mesopotamian plain whose language is often called Assyrian but should technically be referred to as Akkadian. This in turn meant that the second kingdom (from southern Mesopotamia) must be Sumer, and the newly discovered language was therefore 'Sumerian'.

Not all scholars accepted the idea that Sumerian was a distinct language, spoken by a separate racial group. They cited the example of Egyptian hieroglyphics (literally 'holy carvings') which were used to write the same Egyptian language as the demotic script, but are only found on temples and monuments. Hence, they suggested that the Sumerian script was just a 'priestly' form of writing Assyrian. Thus, the very existence of the Sumerians was doubted for many years.

In the meantime, archaeological interest in southern Mesopotamia was heightened by the success of the French diplomat, Ernest de Sarzac, who recovered beautiful stone sculptures of the Sumerian king Gudea from the mound of Tello (ancient Girsu). These discoveries encouraged American, German and British archaeologists to begin work in southern Mesopotamia, and led eventually to the first systematic modern excavations. Some of the most important of these were the German expedition to Uruk (biblical *Erech*), the Anglo-American expedition to Ur (birthplace of Abraham), and the Anglo-Iraqi excavations at Eridu (birthplace of Sumerian civilization). Together, these three cities have given us the earliest archaeological records of the cities and temples of the ancient world.

Chapter 3

The origins of the Temple

Although William Loftus conducted early exploratory digging at Uruk in the mid nineteenth century, the sheer scale of the site was such that only a systematic major excavation program could make a serious attempt at understanding its history. Such a program was pursued by German scholars, on and off, for much of the twentieth century, and has revealed the major architectural phases of Uruk's development.

The most noticeable feature of the landscape of Uruk at the present day is the ruined ziggurat, which dominates the perfectly-flat desert of southern Iraq like a small mountain (Figure 3.1). However, the German excavations showed that the ziggurat itself was built more than a thousand years after the first monumental temple architecture at Uruk, already described in Chapter 1. Incredibly, this early monumental architecture dates back to the prehistoric period, more than 3000 years BC, aptly referred to by Hans Nissen as the Early High Civilization.

Figure 3.1. View of the ruined ziggurat of Uruk at the present day, standing like a small mountain in the flat and desolate landscape of southern Mesopotamia.

According to Sumerian mythology, mankind was created for the sole purpose of serving the gods. Consistent with this stated purpose, the Early High Civilization was centred on the temple, and specifically on the presentation of food and drink offerings to the gods. The operation of the Uruk temple complex must have required huge quantities of such offerings, and evidence suggests that in the prehistoric period, transactions involved in supplying the temple were regulated by means of clay tokens. In this system, each unit of goods, such as a sheep or a jar of oil, was represented by a single token. To make a permanent record of a transaction, the relevant tokens were pressed into a clay ball, which could then be stamped with a seal to officially verify it.

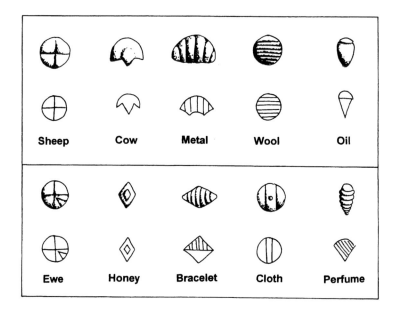

Figure 3.2. Examples of some clay tokens found in Mesopotamian excavations, along with their proto-cuneiform equivalents from archaic bookkeeping records, as proposed by Schmandt-Besserat (1992).

According to the theory of Denise Schmandt-Besserat, the first major development of this accounting system probably occurred at Uruk when the clay tokens previously used to record transactions were replaced by *pictures* of tokens drawn on clay tablets. Some examples of this conversion of tokens into 'pictograms' are shown in Figure 3.2. However, the most important breakthrough was still to come. A member of the Uruk priesthood probably realized that instead of drawing pictures of several sheep tokens to record a day's offering, he could draw a single picture of a sheep token, along with a series of indentations to indicate the quantity. By this simple act, of separating the symbols for number and commodity, the priests of Uruk invented the tools of both counting and writing.

One of the earliest examples of 'proto-cuneiform' writing that can be clearly understood is shown in Figure 3.3. This tablet, bearing an accounting transaction, was found in the Eanna Complex at Uruk, and is estimated to date from around 3300 BC. It records the delivery of two sheep to the temple, shown as a house on a platform (whose sign has been partially obscured by damage). Two other signs reveal the identity of the deity to whom the temple was dedicated. One of these signs (on the left) is a stylized picture of a pole with a loop and streamer, which we know from later cuneiform writing to be the symbol for the goddess Inanna (Akkadian *Ishtar*). The second symbol is a star sign, which means 'heaven' and indicates the divinity of Inanna.

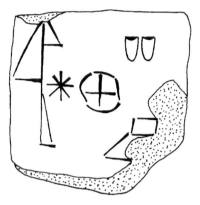

Figure 3.3. Proto-cuneiform tablet from Uruk (excavation level 4) recording the offering of two sheep at the temple of Inanna. The sign for temple is partly lost due to damage. The number '2' is denoted by the double indentation at top-right. Deutsches Archaologisches Institut, University of Heidelberg.

Although the Proto-literate period at Uruk represents the zenith of the Early High Civilization, we can actually trace the development of Sumerian temple building back a further 1500 years, based on excavations at the nearby city of Eridu. This city is attested, both from archaeological evidence and from Sumerian mythology, to be the world's first true city. Furthermore, the excavations, carried out in the late 1940s by Fuad Safar and Seton Lloyd, revealed an amazing series of temple structures, built one above another on a single sacred site.

Mesopotamian excavations can be separated into different levels of occupation because the ancient cities form mounds or 'tells' that have accumulated over periods of thousands of years above the height of the surrounding plain. A view of the inside of an excavated house from Ur gives some clues as to how this happened (Figure 3.4). Only the lower five layers of brick-work used in the walls of this house were built of kiln-fired bricks, whereas the upper parts of the walls were made entirely of sun-dried bricks. Exposed to the elements, these un-baked bricks would have been in a constant state of disintegration, and as clay dust collected in the streets, the ground level in the city would continually rise. To compensate for this process of accumulation, the house shown in Figure 3.4 had a flight of steps leading from street level *down* to the living quarters inside.

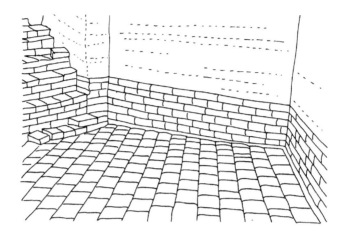

Figure 3.4. Excavated house from the ancient city of Ur, showing a flight of steps from 'street level' down into the house. Based on a photo by Leonard Woolley (1954).

The temples of Eridu can also be separated into different occupation levels, but for slightly different reasons. In this case, the development of the cultic site called for larger and larger temple buildings with the passage of time, leading to frequent rebuilding of these structures. However, the Sumerians clearly regarded the temple site as sacred ground. Therefore, when they planned to build a new temple, they did not completely demolish the old one, but left its foundations intact. These were filled with mud bricks or sand, and were incorporated into a raised platform on which the new temple was built. This meant that over time the temple became elevated on a progressively higher platform . . . the forerunner of the staged tower known in Akkadian as a 'ziggurat'.

As Safar and Lloyd dug down through a total of 19 superimposed temple structures at Eridu, going back through time, the buildings gradually became smaller and simpler until the excavators finally reached a one-room shrine built on a small island in the marsh. Some of the excavated levels are shown in a partially exploded view in Figure 3.5 in order to demonstrate the gradual embellishment of the designs. The very first brick-built temple, at level 19, is thought to date to more than 5000 BC, and marks the earliest architectural remnant of Sumerian civilization.

In order to date successive levels of an excavation such as those shown in Figure 3.5, it is necessary to correlate these levels with the equivalent age of deposits at other excavations. This is done by comparing pottery fragments, which typically show an evolution of form and decoration with time. The prehistoric levels at Eridu and Uruk provide a particularly good example of the pottery dating technique, because it was here in ancient Sumer that one of the most important technological developments in pottery manufacture occurred . . . the invention of the potter's wheel. We know that this development occurred here because of the way

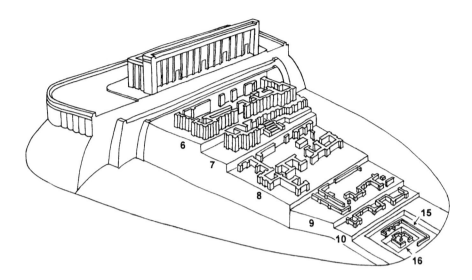

Figure 3.5. Exploded view of consecutive temple ruins at Eridu, going back as far as level 16. Based on an architectural drawing by Heinrich and Seidl (1982).

in which the distinctive styles of Sumerian pottery spread out along the trade routes of the Middle East.

The development of the wheel occurred in two stages, which are reflected in the examples of pottery design illustrated in Figure 3.6 (along with their excavation levels at Eridu and Uruk). The first stage of this development, around 5000 BC, was the invention of the 'Lazy Susan', which permitted a pot to be slowly rotated. This tool was first used to apply decoration to a hand-built pot, and its introduction was marked by a growing prevalence of horizontal ringed decorations around 5000 BC. These could be applied much quicker using the Lazy Susan than the more complex diagonal shapes that had been typical of earlier times. Hence, this represents the world's first 'mass production' technique.

The second stage of development, around 4000 BC, was the fast-turning wheel, which was used to make the world's first wheel-thrown pots. This new tool led to the manufacture of more elaborately *shaped* pots, and for a time, painted decoration was more-or-less dispensed with (Figure 3.6). However, in the Proto-literate period, beginning around 3300 BC, painted decoration of wheel-thrown pots finally came back into fashion. The use of pottery shards provides an excellent method of correlation or *relative* dating between different sites. However, absolute ages for these early deposits must be achieved using radiocarbon dates. These dates are themselves calibrated against tree-rings, in a method termed dendrochronology. Dendrochronology is so accurate that it can potentially give exact yearly ages back to the end of the last Ice Age (around 8,000 BC).

The origins of the Temple

Figure 3.6. Excavation levels at Eridu and Uruk, with representative pottery styles.

Yr BC	Period	Eridu	Uruk	
	Early Dynastic I		1	
3000	~~~~~~~~~~~~~~~~~~~~			
			2	
	Proto-literate		3a	
	(Jemdet Nasr)		3b	
			3c	
3300	~~~~~~~~~~~~~~~~~~~~			
		1	4a	
	Late Uruk		4b	
		2	5	
3600	~~~~~~~~~~~			
			6	
			7	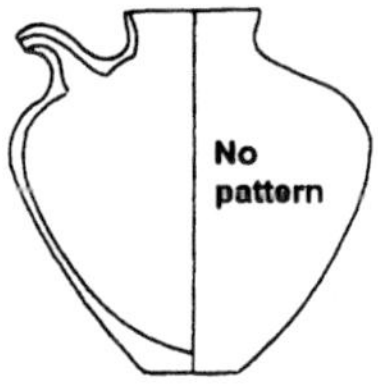
		3	8	
			9	
	Early Uruk		10	No pattern
		4	11	
			12	
			13	
		5	14	
4000	~~~~~~~~~~~~~~~~~~~~			
			15	
		6	16	--------- Ur Flood layer ---------
	Late Ubaid		17	
		7	18	
		8		
	Early Ubaid	9		
		10		
		11		
		12		
	Eridu 2	13		
		14		
5000?				
		15		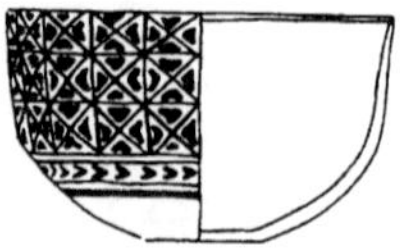
		16		
	Eridu 1	17		
		18		
		19		

In our attempts to understand the evolution of the temple institution at Eridu and Uruk, we are not confined to a study of their ruined foundations. We actually have pictorial images from the Late Uruk period, dating to around 3500 BC, which were found in the temple ruins themselves. These images come from 'cylinder seals'(Figure 3.7), another invention of the Sumerians.

As we have seen, commodity transactions in the prehistoric period could be recorded by pressing tokens into a lump of clay and then stamping them with a seal. The cylinder seal represents a development of the stamp seal, whereby a much larger impression was created by *rolling* the seal across the clay surface. Cylinder seals were typically carved from stone, and are usually about an inch long and half an inch in diameter. Because of their intricate carvings they became a kind of jewellery, often made of semi-precious stone such as jasper or chalcedony. In the example shown in Figure 3.7, the aesthetic appearance of the object was further enhanced by mounting a model of a ram on top of the functional part of the cylinder. The richness of the work suggests that this seal belonged to a very important person, almost certainly a senior member of the priesthood.

Figure 3.7. Cylinder seal of Proto-literate age surmounted by a model of a ram. Height about 4 cm. Ashmolean Museum, Oxford.

The cylinder seal in Figure 3.7 shows buildings set in an agricultural scene, with cows in the upper frieze and calves mingling with buildings in the lower frieze. In addition, calves are depicted on the wall of one building, while another shows clay storage vessels. These depictions imply that the buildings were used for storing agricultural produce. Buildings of remarkably similar design could be seen until recently in the marshlands of southern Mesopotamia (Figure 3.8). These buildings were built by 'Marsh Arabs', who lived near the confluence of the Tigris and Euphrates rivers until the marshes were drained by Saddam Hussein. However, since the fall of his regime, attempts have been made to recreate the marshlands, so that the Marsh Arabs can return to their old way of life.

Figure 3.8. Modern reed-built house typical of those constructed by the Marsh Arabs of southeast Iraq.

The framework of Marsh Arab houses is built from several large bundles of reeds, each bound together with horizontal bands, also made of reeds. This framework forms a series of giant archways that support the walls and roof, along with four large posts at each end of the building (Figure 3.8). The spaces between the framework are then filled in with reed matting, which can be smeared with tar to waterproof it. Examination of the buildings depicted in the cylinder seal shows that they were built in the same way, except that each structure has three posts at the end, and these posts each have three pairs of loops, presumably also made from reeds.

Another ancient cylinder seal, from around 3500 BC at Uruk, provides a link between these early reed-built structures and later brick-built temple architecture. The seal impression (Figure 3.9) shows a temple with ornamented walls, and worshippers approaching by land and water. On either side of the temple is a post with three pairs of loops. The horizontal markings on these posts are clearly reminiscent of the bands used to bind bundles of reeds into the posts of the Marsh Arab houses. However, we also know that the looped post is associated with the Sumerian gods, because a similar post with a single loop became the symbol for the goddess Inanna, as was shown in Figure 3.3.

The brick-built structure shown in Figure 3.9 is probably a good representation of the earliest temples whose foundation remains are seen at Eridu. However, the looped post provides a link to an even earlier style of temple architecture that is no

longer preserved. Because the looped post shows strong evidence of having originated as a bound sheaf of reeds, this suggests that in the earliest period of Sumerian
civilization, temple architecture was built from reeds. Hence, the buildings in Figure
3.9 are probably temple store-houses that recall the beginnings of the tradition of
ritual offerings in ancient Sumer.

Figure 3.9. Impression from an Uruk-age cylinder seal (ca. 3500 BC)
showing an early brick-built temple structure, with a multi-ringed post next
to it. Iraq Museum.

Chapter 4

Searching for the ancient gods

Having observed the centrality and antiquity of the temple in Sumerian civilization, we are led to inquire about the identity of the gods that inspired such devotion. However, this question cannot be answered directly, since the temples described above were built in the prehistoric period, before the invention of writing. Therefore, our strategy will be to examine the pantheon of Mesopotamian gods from later times, and then trace their history back to the earliest periods.

A view of the Mesopotamian pantheon from the post-Sumerian period is provided by a kind of stele (boundary stone) called a *kudurru*. This type of stele first appears during the Kassite period (ca. 1500 BC), but one of the best examples (Figure 4.1) comes from the reign of Nebuchadnezzar I of Babylon, around 1100 BC. The stele has six registers and shows the symbols of the Babylonian gods arranged in a kind of divine hierarchy. Other examples of kudurru show some variation in the composition and hierarchy of the pantheon, but this is one of the most complete. The divine insignia also show minor variations, but we know the meaning of most of them quite well because they were widely used over a long period of time.

At the top of the kudurru in Figure 4.1 are the symbols of the three astral deities, Venus (*Ishtar*), the Moon god (*Sin*) and the Sun god (*Shamash*). Although the Semitic names in italics are widely known, these deities were first worshipped in Sumerian times, when they were known as Inanna, Nanna and Utu respectively. The Moon is shown at the top because the Sun and Venus (the morning star) were regarded as his offspring.

The second register of the stele shows the symbols of another three deities, which are often referred to by scholars as the 'Cosmic Triad' of gods. Each symbol consists of a head-dress made of many sets of superimposed horns (indicative of divinity), resting on a carved altar or throne. The third register also shows three altars, in this case belonging to Marduk god of Babylon (left), the god of writing (middle), and probably the Mother Goddess (right) represented by an umbilical cord. The fourth register shows the gods of war, while the bottom two registers show various other gods and demons. Finally, a large serpent climbs up the edge of the stone (not shown in the figure).

Figure 4.1. Limestone stele from the time of Nebuchadnezzar I, showing
sacred emblems of the gods. Height 56 cm. British Museum.

Although the gods referred to as the Cosmic Triad are in the second register on
the Babylonian kudurru, the literature of ancient Mesopotamia is consistent in
identifying these three gods as the heads of the pantheon during earlier Sumerian
history. These are the God of *Heaven*, the Lord of the *Air,* and the Lord of the
Earth. Hence their title of *Cosmic* Triad, based on the Sumerian concept of the
cosmos, expressed as 'Heaven-Earth'.

All the evidence suggests that the Semitic immigrants to Mesopotamia (the
Akkadians) adopted these gods from the Sumerians, although their names changed
slightly over time. Thus, the God of Heaven, originally named *An* (meaning 'sky'
or 'heaven' in Sumerian) was later pronounced phonetically as *Anu* or *Anna*. On the
other hand, the Lord of the Air, *En-lil* became *El-lil* in Akkadian (since *El* is

Akkadian for 'Lord'). Finally, the Lord of the Earth, *En-ki*, was referred to as *Ea* in Akkadian. (A table summarising the Sumerian and Akkadian names of the major gods is given in Appendix 1).

Despite their slight changes in name, we know that the identity of the Cosmic Triad was the same in Sumerian and Akkadian because their names are written as equivalents in numerous bilingual tablets, and except for Enki-Ea, are written using the same cuneiform signs in both languages. Hence, the continuity of their names allows us to trace the identity of the Cosmic Triad like a golden thread that runs though the whole history of Mesopotamian civilization as it evolved through the millennia (Appendix 2). And if we can follow this thread back far enough, we will learn something about the origins of the pantheon itself.

We begin this quest in the great library of Ashur-banipal, King of Assyria during the 7th century BC. Ashur-banipal was named after his patron-god Ashur, the chief deity of the Assyrian pantheon. He was deeply interested in the priestly literature of ancient Mesopotamia, which was important for the well-being of king and empire because incantation texts and omens were believed to provide their owners with protection against demonic attack. Consequently, Ashur-banipal collected these texts from all of his dominions, and had them transcribed and stored in his great library at Nineveh. When these tablets were copied (Figure 4.2), details

Figure 4.2. Carved wall relief showing an Assyrian scribe holding a clay tablet. British Museum.

of their provenance and the process of transcription were often contained in a title at the end of the tablet called a 'colophon'. Some of the tablets in the library even claim that the king himself was involved in their copying. For example:

> I wrote on the tablets the wisdom of Nabu (god of writing) . . .
> I checked and collated them.
> I placed them for posterity in the library of the temple of my lord Nabu . . .
> In Nineveh, for my life, for the guarding of my soul,
> That I might not have illness,
> And for making firm the foundation of my royal throne . . .
> [Translation: Saggs, 2000]

Although Ashur-banipal claimed the ability to read and write, this was a skill that most rulers of his day probably lacked, because of the extreme complexity of the cuneiform writing system. As noted earlier, this system of writing had been invented around 3500 BC, probably at Uruk, for the purpose of keeping temple records on clay tablets. In its original form, a series of objects were each represented by a drawing, such as a sketch of a human head (Figure 4.3). However, as the script evolved, the drawings became more and more stylized, and later even turned on their sides. This evolution is shown in Figure 4.3, and demonstrates that by the 7th century BC, the cuneiform script had become completely abstract.

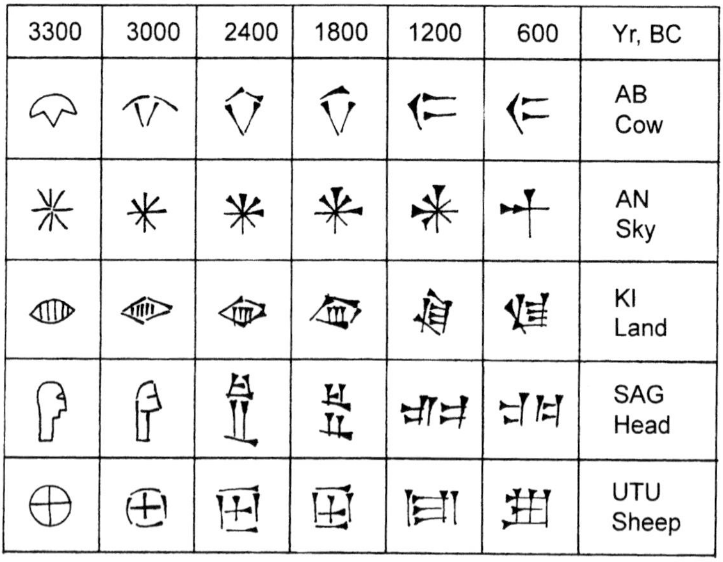

3300	3000	2400	1800	1200	600	Yr, BC
						AB Cow
						AN Sky
						KI Land
						SAG Head
						UTU Sheep

Figure 4.3. Evolution of cuneiform signs from early pictographic forms to late abstract forms around the time of Ashur-banipal. Note that the signs became turned on their side sometime after 1800 BC (ages approximate).

In addition to evolving in style, cuneiform signs also evolved in their usage, from a series of separate pictures to a phonetic system where each sign represented a particular sound in the Sumerian (and later the Akkadian) language. This allowed the writing of names and abstract concepts, so that by 2500 BC, cuneiform could be used to write works of literature. However, the old pictographic writing system continued to exist alongside the new phonetic system. This made cuneiform writing both complex and ambiguous, so that definitive understandings of inscriptions could (and can) only be obtained after many years of study.

The library of Ashur-banipal probably consisted of two different collections, since the colophons of some tablets speak of a royal library, whereas others speak of the library of the Temple of Nabu (god of writing). However, both collections were assembled at the Assyrian capital by Ashur-banipal. A small part of this material was discovered by Layard in 1850, during his second expedition to Meso-potamia. However, the main collection was discovered three years later by Hor-muzd Rassam, originally Layard's assistant but later his successor, working under the overall supervision of Henry Rawlinson in Baghdad.

In December 1853, Rassam began digging in the area now known as the North Palace at Nineveh. The work was begun in secret because Rawlinson had earlier given French archaeologists permission to dig in this area. However, the French had been busy at nearby Khorsabad, so Rassam took the chance of 'invading' the French area at Nineveh. On the third night of digging, Rassam discovered a magnif-icent bas-relief wall panel five feet high, showing King Ashur-banipal leading the royal lion hunt (Figure 4.4). Having thus made a major find, Rassam was confident that Rawlinson would now support his 'claim' to excavate this part of the mound. This proved correct, and the French reluctantly accepted the *fait accompli*.

Figure 4.4. Carved bas-relief from Nineveh showing Ashur-banipal lead-ing the lion hunt. British Museum.

When Rassam's workmen dug trenches to follow the line of the wall relief, they discovered that it was part of a set of reliefs that told the complete story of the royal lion hunt. These were set round the walls of a chamber that turned out to be the great hall of the royal palace. However, when Rassam started to clear the middle of the chamber he was puzzled to find a vast number of clay tablets in chaotic piles. He was not particularly interested in the tablets, but fortunately gave instructions that they should be collected up and packed in boxes for shipment to the British Museum. The presence of a major archive in the middle of the great hall was very puzzling, but it was later suggested that the royal library was located on the floor above the great hall and collapsed down into it when the palace was sacked and burned.

The tablets excavated by Rassam, along with the best of the wall reliefs, were shipped back to London in 1855, the same year that Rawlinson left Baghdad for the last time. They eventually found their way to the British Museum, where the tablets remained packed in the basement for many years. Finally, an informal group of self-taught scholars began to study these tablets under the direction of Rawlinson and the Curator of Western Asiatic Antiquities, Samuel Birch. One of the 'amateur scholars' in this group was George Smith, a trainee engraver who was given a minor position at the museum in recognition of his devoted interest in cuneiform inscriptions.

Smith's job was to sort the tablets and fragments from Ashur-banipal's library into different categories of subject matter, and if possible, to join together broken fragments. The category of greatest interest was 'mythological', and after the initial work of sorting was completed, Smith began to study these tablets in more detail. It was while examining this material that Smith came across several fragments that he recognized as a Mesopotamian account of the Great Flood described in Genesis (Figure 4.5).

In 1872, Smith announced his discovery in a lecture to the Biblical Archaeology Society which was attended by a distinguished gathering of London society, including the Prime Minister himself. At this lecture Smith translated several excerpts of the Mesopotamian Flood Story, pointing out the remarkable resemblances between the Mesopotamian and biblical accounts. For example, both versions describe how the Flood Hero sent out a series of birds to test the abating of the waters after the Flood (Gen 8:6-12). These detailed similarities showed beyond any doubt that the biblical and Mesopotamian versions of the Flood Story came from a common source.

Smith continued to gather tablets which seemed to have parallels with the Genesis text, and in 1876 he published his great work '*The Chaldean Account of Genesis (containing the description of the Creation, the Fall of Man, the Deluge, the Tower of Babel, the Times of the Patriarchs and Nimrod, Babylonian fables and legends of the gods from the cuneiform inscriptions)*'. There were many gaps in the Mesopotamian account, but it appeared that with time these would eventually be filled, providing an 'original' account of primaeval history from which the Genesis account must have been derived.

Figure 4.5. The largest fragment of the Mesopotamian Flood Story, from
the eleventh tablet of the *Epic of Gilgamesh*. British Museum.

This view was reinforced by the events surrounding the *Daily Telegraph*
expedition of 1873. This newspaper volunteered to fund an expedition by Smith to
Nineveh in order for him to look for missing fragments of the Flood Story. After
many setbacks, Smith eventually reached Nineveh and began to re-excavate debris
from the great hall where the library of Ashur-banipal had been found. Incredibly,
Smith had been at the site less than a week when he found a fragment bearing one
of the largest missing parts of the story. However, he was even more astonished
when he read his published report, in a copy of the *Daily Telegraph* that reached
him in the field. Seemingly the report had been doctored by the paper's editors,
because Smith read of his intention to terminate the excavation, "as the season is
closing"! Thus out-manoeuvred, Smith had no alternative but to return home.
However, he was eventually sent back to Nineveh by the British Museum and
recovered many other important tablets.

It is now known that much of the material attributed to the *Chaldean Account
of Genesis* actually comprises parts of two completely separate epic works which
we refer to as the *Epic of Gilgamesh* and the *Babylonian Creation Epic*. The
Creation Epic is actually mainly concerned with titanic battles for supremacy

between the gods. It contains a brief account of the creation of the Heavens and the Earth, but does not mention the Flood or the Garden of Eden. On the other hand the *Gilgamesh Epic* lacks a creation story but deals with these other themes as it describes the hero's quest for the secret of immortality.

The discovery that the 'Genesis' fragments were part of two different epics showed that the account of the Creation and Flood in Genesis could not be based directly on a single Mesopotamian source. However, if we are able to trace the thread of the Cosmic Triad back through the history of Mesopotamian literature, we may discover the origins of both the Mesopotamian and the biblical view of the gods.

Chapter 5

The history of the Pantheon

At the time of Ashur-banipal (650 BC), the literature of ancient Mesopotamia already stretched back almost 2000 years into the mists of time. Even the most recent of the epics in the Great Library (the *Babylonian Creation Epic*) was more than 400 years old, and looked back to a period before the Assyrian empire had even been founded. Leonard King made the first relatively complete translation of the Creation Epic in 1902, referring to it as the *Seven Tablets of Creation*. However, it is more commonly referred to by its first two words in Akkadian, *Enuma Elish* ('When above . . .').

The *Enuma Elish* was written in Akkadian, probably around 1100 BC, during the reign of Nebuchadnezzar I of Babylon. It was composed as a liturgical epic to celebrate the ascendancy of the god Marduk to his position as the head of the Mesopotamian pantheon. Marduk was originally an obscure god from Babylon, and first rose to prominence when Hammurabi conquered Mesopotamia around 1750 BC. He continued to grow in importance through the Second Millennium, finally becoming the undisputed head of the Mesopotamian pantheon in the reign of Nebuchadnezzar I. (It was only much later that Marduk himself was ousted as head of the pantheon by Ashur, the chief god of the Assyrians). The depiction of Marduk in Figure 5.1 shows him riding on his dragon serpent and holding the 'looped rod' that is a symbol of divine authority. This symbol is probably derived from the looped poles that were the marks of the earliest Sumerian divinities (Figures 3.7 and 3.9).

The Creation Epic begins by recounting the 'family tree' of Marduk, in which two gods of the Cosmic Triad (Anu and Enki) appear as Marduk's grand-father and father respectively. The epic then goes on to describe a great battle between the gods, culminating in the triumph of Marduk over the sea goddess Tiamat. After slicing her in two, Marduk proceeds to create the heavens and earth from the two halves of Tiamat's corpse. However, before making the Tigris and Euphrates flow from her eye-sockets, and long before the creation of mankind, one of Marduk's first acts is to establish cult centres for Anu, Enlil and Enki. This provides unwitting evidence for the earlier prominence of these gods of the Cosmic Triad, whose place (by 1100 BC) had been usurped by Marduk.

Figure 5.1. Depiction of the god Marduk on part of a lapis lazuli cylinder designed to be hung around the neck of the god's cult statue. Berlin Museum.

The *Epic of Gilgamesh* is a very different work from *Enuma Elish*, being more of an adventure story than a temple liturgy. Its theme is the heroism of man in the face of adversity, and it describes the vain quest of the hero Gilgamesh for the lost secret of eternal life (Figure 5.2). Despite its strong plot development, the epic was not composed as a 'new work', but was woven together from several much older short stories. We know this because Sumerian versions of several of these stories have been found in a much older temple library at Nippur, dating from the Old Babylonian period (ca. 1600 BC). The Flood Story is one of these earlier works, and does not involve Gilgamesh directly. However, it was included in the epic on the pretext of the Flood Hero explaining to Gilgamesh how he was given the gift of eternal life by the gods. Consequently, in this version of the story, the Flood Hero is called Ut-napishtim, meaning 'he found life'.

In the Flood Story of the *Gilgamesh Epic*, the three gods of the Cosmic Triad are pre-eminent, and Marduk is not even mentioned. Instead, we find Anu and Enlil presiding over the court of the gods, while Enki acts as the divine advocate for mankind. When Enki discovers the plan of Anu and Enlil to destroy mankind in a flood, he secretly communicates the plan of the gods to Ut-napishtim by whispering (like the wind) through the walls of a reed hut. By this means Enki gives instructions on how to build an Ark to survive the Flood, and Ut-napishtim obeys the divine command. After surviving the Flood, Ut-napishtim is rewarded for his obedience to Enki and is sent to a land of immortality at the ends of the earth. According to the Sumerian version of the Flood Story from Nippur, this land was in the east, on an island mountain called Dilmun.

Figure 5.2. Impression of an Akkadian cylinder seal, possibly showing the quest of Gilgamesh and his sparring-partner Enkidu for the Tree of Life (centre). British Museum.

Going back nearly 1000 years before the amassing of the great library of Ashur-banipal, the *Epic of Atrahasis*, dating from the Old Babylonian period, provides the theological background to the creation of mankind in *Enuma Elish*, and also to the Flood Story in the *Gilgamesh Epic*. Only small fragments of the *Atrahasis Epic* were discovered at Nineveh, but a relatively complete Old Babylonian version was discovered at Sippar, near present-day Baghdad.

The epic begins with a riot in heaven, when a group of 'working gods' rebel (Figure 5.3) against the heavy labour decreed by the great gods, of digging and repairing irrigation ditches. This work began with the digging of the Tigris and Euphrates, and continued for 3600 years (almost an eternity) until the gods could bear it no longer. Therefore the rebel gods surrounded the temple of Enlil, counsellor of the gods, to bring their complaint. The vizier of Enlil then suggests sending for the other two members of the Cosmic Triad to get their assistance in dealing with the riot.

Figure 5.3. Gods fighting amongst themselves (their divinity indicated by their horned head-dresses). Impression of an Akkadian cylinder seal from Kish. Metropolitan Museum of Art, New York.

When they arrive, Anu proposes to send the vizier of Enlil to meet with the rebels to ascertain the nature of their grievance. After hearing the complaint, Enlil proposes that one of the lesser gods will be executed as an example to the others. However, Enki, god of wisdom, proposes a better solution. He will take the blood of the slaughtered god and mix it with wet clay to create mankind. The flesh of the dead god will beat in the breast of mankind to provide him with his life-giving spirit, and mankind will then serve the gods and relieve them of their work.

This plan seemed good to the gods, but unfortunately, as mankind grew in numbers, he made so much noise that the sleep of Enlil was disturbed. Enlil made several attempts to destroy humanity (the final attempt being the Great Flood). However, each attempt was thwarted when Enki revealed a way of escape to a devout worshipper. In this version of the epic, the Flood Hero is named Extra-wise (*Atrahasis*) because of his wisdom in building the Ark according to Enki's instructions. His name has been used in modern times to entitle the epic, but it was known to the ancients by its first line, *Enuma ilu awilum* (When the gods like men . . .).

Going back another 1000 years, to the Early Dynastic period, we come to the dawn of literature itself. Around 2600 BC, the very earliest Sumerian literature consists of one or two temple hymns, and the world's earliest collection of proverbs, which pre-date the biblical Book of Proverbs by more than 1500 years. These Sumerian proverbs are referred to as the *Instructions of Shuruppak*, because they are supposed to represent advice given by the king of Shuruppak to his son, none other than the pious Atrahasis.

The ancient city of Shuruppak seems to have been a centre of Sumerian scholarship, with one of the world's first scribal schools. One of the principal methods by which scribes learned the art of writing was the copying of various kinds of tablets, which formed a kind of 'standard curriculum' of Sumerian texts. Many of the practice copies of the students have been preserved in piles of garbage, where they were tossed when the lesson was over. These texts represent a vital legacy for the modern scholar because the texts in the curriculum were reproduced verbatim for hundreds of years after their original composition. For example, the *Instructions of Shuruppak* were first written in archaic Sumerian cuneiform, which consisted only of strings of words with little or no grammatical construction. However, the surviving fragments of the ancient version can be matched up with well-preserved Old Babylonian versions, written a thousand years later, which are well understood.

Another important part of the scribal curriculum was a collection of ordered 'word lists'. The most famous is the *Standard List of Professions* (Figure 5.4), which lists dozens of occupations in a descending order of importance, beginning with the ancient equivalent of the king. The significance of this document is that it can be traced back in time from a 'mature' version, written around 2600 BC, to a 'proto-cuneiform' version written 500 years earlier, during the Proto-literate period. Word lists are very important for the decipherment of proto-cuneiform signs because they link these signs to the recognized cuneiform of later literature. However, these word lists can also provide a window into the world of ancient Sumer from hundreds of years before the first historical or literary texts.

One type of list that is important for tracing the history of the pantheon is the 'god list'. The first part of such a list, also from ancient Shuruppak, is shown in

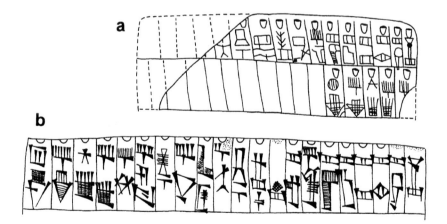

Figure 5.4. The beginning of the *Standard List of Professions*, a) from ca. 3100 BC (Freie Universitat, Berlin); b) from ca. 2600 BC (Oriental Institute, Chicago). The first twenty-one entries are shown in their ancient orientation (before the rotation of tablets that later occurred) and are read from right to left.

Figure 5.5. The tablet is read in panels from right to left, and the first two such panels express the cuneiform names of En-lil and En-ki. However, each panel actually contains three signs (in addition to the semi-circular 'bullet' which itemizes each entry in many word lists). The star sign, which is the first character in each panel, is not part of the name, but is an 'identifier', signifying divinity, which is pronounced in Sumerian as *dingir.*

However, a major problem with the 'god list' is that, unlike most other scribal teaching lists, the order of the entries is not fixed. In fact, several different god lists are known from various cities, and of various ages. The gods of the Cosmic Triad usually appear in the first half-dozen entries, but there is a surprising degree of variation, even in tablets of the same age from one city (for example, ancient Shuruppak). This variability led a prominent French scholar to remark that *'Sumerian religion presents itself to our eyes like a monster with a hundred different heads'* (my translation from the French).

Figure 5.5. The beginning of a god list from Shuruppak. Vatican Museum.

Paradoxically, we can make more sense of early Sumerian religion (before 3000 BC) by examining another important type of list, the *Archaic City List*, rather than the God List. Like the *Standard List of Professions*, the City List has been found in deposits dating to around 2600 BC (Early Dynastic) as well as 3100 BC (Proto-literate). Also like the *Standard List of Professions*, the City List is preserved in the same order in these two examples separated by 500 years of history (Figure 5.6). However, the City List is also found in several partially-complete cylinder seal impressions. When Roger Matthews used these impressions to reconstruct the original cylinder seal, he again found the same order of cities, with one small exception (the reversal of Larsa and Nippur).

The City List is important for understanding early Sumerian religion because of the association of different gods of the pantheon with specific cities. Throughout the history of Sumerian civilization in the Third Millennium (3000 - 2000 BC), each of these cities had a different patron god (or occasionally more than one god). For example, Ur was always associated with the Moon god, Larsa with the Sun god, Uruk with the God of heaven (and also Inanna, Queen of heaven), Nippur with En-lil, and Eridu with En-ki.

The lists in Figure 5.6 confirm the great antiquity of this association between cities and gods. We can see this by comparing the cuneiform signs for a city and its patron god. For example, the written form of the city of Larsa is a schematic picture of a temple on top of a ziggurat, along with a picture of the rising sun (ie 'temple of the sun'). Similarly, the cuneiform for Utu, god of Larsa, is also a picture of the rising sun, but preceded by the star sign to indicate divinity (ie 'the divine sun'). These links show that Larsa was associated with the Sun god from the earliest development of proto-cuneiform signs (ca. 3500 BC). We know this because the written signs are pictograms, schematically illustrating a scene. They do not correspond phonetically to the sounds of '*Larsa*' or '*Utu*'.

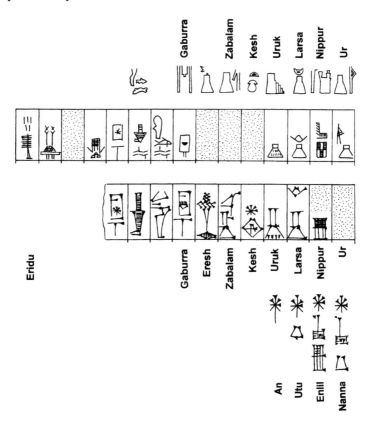

Figure 5.6. The beginning of the *Archaic City List* from a cylinder seal (top), and Proto-literate and Early Dynastic tablets (middle), compared with the cuneiform signs of four patron gods (bottom). Entries 2 and 3 on the seal have been reversed. Shading = damaged areas. Based on drawings by Matthews (1993), Englund and Nissen (1993) and Biggs (1974).

Another direct correspondence is seen in Figure 5.6 between the city of Nippur and its god En-lil. Here the written form of *En-lil means 'the divine Lord of the Air', while the cuneiform signs for the city are exactly the same, (literally, *En-lil*), but without the star sign.

The final correspondence that is of particular interest in Figure 5.6 is that between the God of Heaven and the city of Uruk. In this case, the city is designated by a temple on a ziggurat, but without any other sign, except that the ziggurat itself is ornamented with small tick marks. On the seal, the equivalent to this ornamentation appears to be a series of small steps, which may represent the actual stairway used by the priests to ascend to the temple on top of the ziggurat. The conclusion that we may draw is that the ziggurat of Uruk was the archetypal temple on a high platform, after which all subsequent ziggurats were modelled. The best preserved of these later ziggurats, at Ur, has been partially restored in modern times, and is shown as a reconstruction in Figure 5.7.

Figure 5.7. Artist's impression of the original appearance of the great ziggurat of Ur, showing the grand stairway used by the priests to ascend to the house of the god. Based on a reconstruction by Woolley (1939).

Returning to the cuneiform signs in Figure 5.6, we can see that just as the city of Uruk was written with a single sign, so also its patron god An (or Anu) was represented by a star with no other sign. In fact *An* is simply the Sumerian word for heaven or sky. The fact that his sign became the archaetypal symbol of divinity (*dingir* in Sumerian or *ilu* in Akkadian) provides powerful evidence from the dawn of written history that indeed An was the Father of the Gods, as claimed in later mythology. However, as Sumerian civilization evolved, and the gods of the pantheon multiplied, the God of Heaven became less and less distinctive as a deity and his star sign became a general word for any god. This meant that when his name was written in Akkadian or later Sumerian texts, another sign was added after the star sign to make the phonetic rendering '*An-u*' or '*An-na*'. This was now necessary to distinguish the name of the God of Heaven from the generic identifier of any god. So, from being the pre-eminent god of the universe, Anu now became just one god amongst a whole pantheon of competing deities.

Chapter 6

Rivalry between the gods

One name that has been notably absent from this discussion of the City List is Eridu, yet archaeological evidence discussed above suggests that the temple of Eridu was the first centre of institutional worship in ancient Sumer, preceding the temples of Uruk by as much as a thousand years. However, several lines of evidence suggest that Uruk superceded Eridu as the pre-eminent religious centre of ancient Sumer sometime after 4000 BC. This 'transfer' of spiritual authority from Eridu to Uruk is recalled in a Sumerian myth that describes how the 'decrees of civilization' were carried from Eridu to Uruk.

Figure 6.1. A banqueting scene, depicted using an inlay of shell and lapis lazuli in pitch. The size of each figure signifies their social importance, with the king seated on the left. Enlarged from the 'Standard of Ur' from the Early Dynastic royal tombs of Ur. British Museum.

According to this myth, Inanna, goddess of Uruk and consort of Anu, goes to visit her 'father' Enki in the hope of obtaining the decrees of civilization from him. Enki invites Inanna to a banquet (Figure 6.1), where he becomes intoxicated, and in a display of kingly liberality, starts to present the decrees to Inanna. Altogether, Enki presents Inanna with over a hundred decrees, governing all aspects of Sumerian civilization. She then loads them on her 'boat of heaven' and quickly departs for Uruk with the precious cargo. When Enki has sobered up, he notices with alarm that the decrees are missing. He questions his vizier Isimud and is told that he himself presented the decrees to Inanna during the banquet. Greatly upset, Enki sends Isimud and a group of sea-monsters after Inanna to try to stop her before she can reach Uruk. There are seven stopping places where Isimud intercepts Inanna, but at each one she is rescued by her vizier, Nin-shubar. Finally she arrives safely at the quay-side of Uruk and unloads the decrees, to the jubilation of the inhabitants.

The key element in this story is the fact that the supremacy of Uruk over Eridu was secured by Inanna (Queen of Heaven), rather than by Anu, God of Heaven. In fact, as well as achieving supremacy over Enki, Inanna seems also to have usurped the place of Anu himself. This is suggested by a kind of 'spiritual arms race' that took place between two different temple complexes in Uruk over the period from around 3500 to 3000 BC. Of these two complexes, the so called 'Anu ziggurat' was dedicated to the God of Heaven, whereas the Eanna Complex (literally 'House of Heaven') was dedicated to Inanna, (literally 'Lady of Heaven' or 'Nin-anna'). The rivalry between the two complexes in the late Fourth Millennium seems to be reflected by very frequent episodes of temple demolition and rebuilding. At each stage, the temple platforms were made higher and the buildings on them larger and more elaborate, as first one and then the other priestly faction achieved political supremacy.

The rivalry between the two temple complexes may also have been responsible for innovations in temple architecture and construction seen during this period. These innovations include the introduction of limestone foundations to replace the

Figure 6.2. Restoration of part of a row of joined columns from around 3300 BC at Uruk, showing the spectacular appearance of cone-mosaic decoration. Pergamon Museum, Berlin.

brick in earlier use, the development of the world's first columned walkway, and the invention of spectacular new forms of decoration. For example, the designers of the Eanna Complex invented 'cone-mosaic' decoration, by which coloured cones were pressed into mud-plastered walls to produce spectacular patterned designs (Figure 6.2). To outdo this effect, the temple of the Anu ziggurat was plastered with powdered gypsum, so that it would sparkle brilliantly in the Mesopotamian sunshine.

The ascendancy of Inanna at Uruk was based on her role as the goddess of the store-house. This role is illustrated on the famous Uruk Vase, one of the most important artifacts that was stolen from the Iraq Museum after the 2003 war, but fortunately later recovered. This one-metre-high carved alabaster vase was excavated from the Proto-literate levels of the Eanna Complex at Uruk, and shows the presentation of offerings at the temple of Inanna (Figure 6.3). The vase has four registers, but the upper one is the most important for its detailed illustration of the presentation scene.

Figure 6.3. View of the Uruk Vase to show the four registers of the bas-relief design. Iraq Museum, Baghdad.

Beginning briefly with the lower registers, the bottom one contains a frieze of alternating palm trees and wheat stalks growing next to water (represented by a wavy line). Above a narrow horizontal band, the next register shows alternating goats and sheep. Taken together, these two registers summarize the agricultural economy of Uruk, consisting of stock, grain, and date harvesting. The third register shows naked men, presumed to be priests, bringing harvest products in open baskets, open clay vessels, and clay jars (presumably containing oil or wine). Finally, the large upper register shows the presentation of these gifts at the sanctuary.

The upper register of the Uruk Vase is flattened out in Figure 6.4 to show the details of the presentation scene at the temple. The entrance to the shrine is marked by two looped door-posts, indicating its dedication to Inanna. Behind the entrance is a bull (probably a statue) and two tables bearing human figurines, which are probably cult statues. Behind these statues is another looped post, indicating a separate storeroom. This contains the stored fruits of the harvest in jars, along with pictures of animals probably representing stored meat. In front of the shrine stands a female figure in a long bordered gown. She appears to be wearing a horned head-dress, indicating her divinity, although this part of the pot was damaged and repaired in antiquity, so the head-dress is unclear. Nevertheless, even without this evidence, the female figure must either be a goddess, or a priestess representing her.

Figure 6.4. Detailed view of the upper register of the Uruk Vase, flattened out to show the presentation of offerings at the temple storehouse. Iraq Museum, Baghdad.

Facing the priestess or goddess are three figures. The first, resembling the naked priests on the register below, bears a large vessel of fruit, probably dates. The second figure is largely missing, due to a substantial area of damage, but we can see that the (smaller) third figure, who is female, is holding the train of a heavy bordered gown. This indicates that the second figure is a person of high status. However, at this early stage in Sumerian civilization, the office of secular kingship had not yet appeared. Therefore, this figure is interpreted as a male god, or his representative, the high priest.

Thorkild Jacobsen, one of the greatest Sumerologists of the 20th century, argued that the scene on the Uruk Vase represents the personification of an ancient fertility cult. By this process of personification, the entry of the harvest into the store-room was represented as a relationship between two gods. The harvest, personified as the god Dumuzi, enters into the storehouse, personified as the goddess Inanna, leading to a 'sacred marriage' between them. Sumerian and Babylonian literature make it clear that in the ritual of Sacred Marriage the gods were 'impersonated' by priest-esses and either priests or kings, and that the rite was sexually consummated.

Evidence from cylinder seals suggests that the worship of the Sun god also developed from a fertility cult. For example, the seal impression in Figure 6.5 shows the Sun god Utu in his 'boat of heaven' with agricultural symbols, including a plough and a goddess of the fields. This suggests that veneration of the Sun god originated as a cult of agricultural fertility. Similarly, the Moon god Nanna probably originated in another fertility cult, based on the role of the moon in marking the female menstrual cycle, as well as the agricultural seasons. At the same time, the promotion of Inanna from goddess of the storehouse to Queen of Heaven was symbolized by her identification as Venus, the morning and evening star.

Figure 6.5. Impression of an Akkadian cylinder seal, showing the Sun god in his 'boat of heaven' associated with symbols of agricultural fertility. Bibliothèque National, Paris.

By this process of association, fertility cults at the cities of Ur, Larsa, and Uruk probably evolved into a triad of astral gods, Nanna, Utu, and Inanna, which rivalled the Cosmic Triad of Anu, Enlil and Enki. The success of the 'Astral Triad' in the Babylonian period is demonstrated by their position at the head of the kudurru stele (Figure 3.1). However, the *early* (Fourth Millennium BC) ascendancy of the Astral Triad, to rival the Cosmic Triad, is demonstrated by the prominent place of Ur, Larsa and Uruk at the beginning of the Proto-literate City List, reflecting the early proliferation of gods and goddesses in the Sumerian pantheon.

The eclipse of Eridu by Uruk is demonstrated by the placing of Eridu in only the fifteenth position in the *Archaic City List*. Thus, by the late Fourth Millennium, Eridu had obviously sunk to second-rank status amongst the cities of the plain. However, although this change in status was explained in Sumerian mythology by the transfer of the decrees of civilization from Eridu to Uruk, scientific evidence suggests that it was actually caused by environmental changes. For example, archaeological evidence from Eridu suggests that around 3500 BC the subsidiary buildings around the temple were abandoned and filled by blown sand. The timing of this decline ties in with evidence of changing environmental conditions around the middle of the Fourth Millennium, involving the drying of the regional climate and the encroachment of the sea towards Eridu.

Eridu had originally been near a freshwater lake, but was not on the main channel of the Euphrates River. Hence, if the water supply from the lake was compromised by drought or by contamination with sea-water, this would have caused salination of the soil, reducing agricultural production. To offset these effects, a canal was dug to link Eridu to the main river. However, the city of Uruk was already located on the main channel of the Euphrates, 70 km upstream of Eridu (Figure 6.6). This would have provided more plentiful access to water, giving Uruk an advantage during drier climatic conditions. Indeed, practically all of the prominent cities of Sumerian civilization were situated on the ancient channels of the Tigris or Euphrates, as shown in Figure 6.6. Hence the transition between climatic periods probably corresponds to the time when Uruk eclipsed Eridu in importance as the leading city of Sumer.

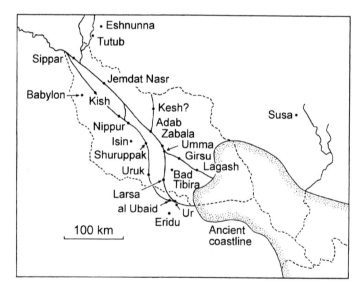

Figure 6.6. Map of Mesopotamia showing the distribution of most Third Millennium cities along major ancient channels of the Tigris and Euphrates (modern river channels and coastline are dashed).

Chapter 7

The King List and the Flood

As we have already seen in Chapter 3, archaeology provides one source of evidence for the primacy of Eridu in the early development of ancient Sumer. However, we must now examine the other main source of evidence for the early importance of Eridu, which is the *Sumerian King List*. Copies of this inscription have been found in several Sumerian cities, but the most complete version is the Weld-Blundell prism (Figure 7.1), which begins with a list of eight kings who ruled before the Flood and ends with the Isin dynasty of the Old Babylonian period (Appendix 2).

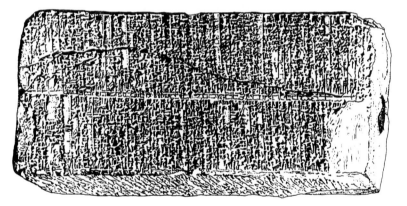

Figure 7.1. The Weld-Blundell prism shown in the orientation in which the ancient cuneiform script might have been read. Ashmolean Museum, Oxford.

The King List was probably first composed around 2100 BC, and describes a succession of dynasties from a much earlier time that were supposed to have ruled over the whole Mesopotamian plain in consecutive periods. It is one of the few sources in Mesopotamian literature that somewhat resembles a historical document; however, its main purpose was to demonstrate the antiquity and continuity of Sumerian civilization, rather than to provide a chronological record. For example, many of the dynasties after the Flood are thought to have been partially overlapping, rather than consecutive. However, this does not necessarily mean that the compilers of the King List were ignorant of their past or intent on misrepresenting it. Rather, we should see their work as constrained by the archival principles of their age.

When the King List was first composed, Sumerian civilization had recently been restored from more than two hundred years of repression and anarchy. This period began when the Semitic king, Sargon of Akkad, conquered all of Mesopotamia around 2350 BC. Sargon and his grand-son Naram-Sin were great warriors, and built the world's first empire, stretching from the Persian Gulf to the Mediterranean. However, after achieving these victories, Naram-Sin desecrated the temple of Enlil at Nippur by demolishing its sanctuary. According to a Sumerian lamentation called the *Curse of Akkad*, this sacrilege was punished by Enlil, who allowed the plains to be invaded by barbarians from the Iranian mountains. The century of anarchy which followed was finally brought to an end by the re-establishment of a Sumerian dynasty at Ur.

Table 7.1. Summary of dynasties in the *Sumerian King List* up to the end of the Early Dynastic period. After Finegan (1979).

Name of Dynasty		Number of kings	Total length of reigns, yr
Eridu		2	64,800
Bad-Tibira		3	108,000
Larak		1	28,800
Sippar		1	21,000
Shuruppak		1	18,600
~~The Flood~~~~~~~~~~~~~~~~			
Kish	1	23	24,510
Uruk	1	12	2,310
Ur	1	4	177
Awan		3	356
Kish	2	8	3,195
Hamazi		1	360
Uruk	2	3	187
Ur	2	4	116
Adab		1	90
Mari		6	136
Kish	3	1 (queen)	100
Akshak		6	99
Kish	4	7	491
Uruk	3	1	25

In order to emphasize the continuity of the new dynasty with the glories of earlier Sumerian civilization, the compilers of the King List joined together a series of ancient king lists which they had inherited (either in written or verbal form) to create a coherent document. The theme of their chronicle was the passing of the 'torch' of civilization from one city to another through history. In reality, different city states often co-existed for lengthy periods before one or the other gained overall supremacy. However, rather than omit overlapping dynasties from their account, the compilers of the King List just joined them end-to-end to create a stylized history of Sumerian civilization. The resulting succession of dynasties is summarized in Table 7.1.

One of the most important overlapping sections in the King List is between the first dynasties of Kish and Uruk respectively. The King List names the hero Gilgamesh as the fifth king in the latter dynasty. However, Sumerian epic tales also link Gilgamesh to a contemporary king from Kish, Me-baragesi, who was the penultimate ruler of his dynasty. The crucial thing about this linkage is that Me-baragesi himself is attested as 'King of Kish' by one of the earliest contemporary inscriptions. The archaic cuneiform signs in this inscription (Figure 7.2a) are read vertically downwards and from right to left. The first three signs (at right) represent a phonetic spelling of the king's name. The middle sign is a stylized view of a man with a crown on his head, meaning 'king', while the left-hand character (partly missing) is the cuneiform sign for Kish.

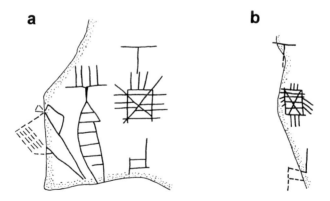

Figure 7.2. Drawings of the some of the earliest known contemporary royal inscriptions. a) Iraq Museum. b) Oriental Institute, Chicago.

Unfortunately, this inscription was purchased on the antiquities market rather than excavated, and therefore has no provenance. However, a less complete version bearing only the king's name was found on a fragment of a carved stone vessel in the temple at Tutub (Figure 7.2b). The good agreement between the style of the two inscriptions helps to verify the one without provenance. The age of the deposit containing the stone vessel (ca. 2500 BC) is only slightly younger than the estimated date of Gilgamesh based on the King List (ca. 2640 BC). The latter estimate was made by Thorkild Jacobsen, assuming an average duration of 25 years for each kingly reign, and bearing in mind the overlapping nature of many of the dynasties. The consistency between these two separate lines of evidence therefore provides strong support for the overall accuracy of the King List, especially when we consider that these kings reigned hundreds of years before the list was compiled.

Further support for the accuracy of the King List comes from archaeological evidence for the existence of a royal palace at Kish, dated to around 2700 BC. The foundation plan of this royal palace (Figure 7.3) exhibits a style of architecture that is distinct from the earlier temple buildings of ancient Sumer. Hence, these remains provide the first evidence for the establishment of the office of a secular king who was distinct from the temple hierarchy. This kingship evidently dominated the whole of Sumer for a long time, generating immense prestige, because subsequent dynasties who conquered the plain declared their supremacy by titling themselves as 'King of Kish'.

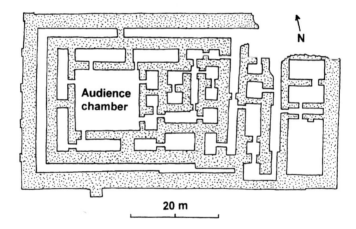

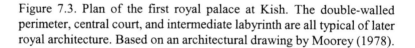

Figure 7.3. Plan of the first royal palace at Kish. The double-walled perimeter, central court, and intermediate labyrinth are all typical of later royal architecture. Based on an architectural drawing by Moorey (1978).

According to the most complete versions of the King List, kingship was instituted by the gods twice; once at the beginning of human civilization (at Eridu), and once after the Flood (at Kish). We have seen that the dynasty of Kish is verified by archaeological evidence. However, the earlier primacy of Eridu is more sketchily understood. For example, the King List advertises its own uncertainty about these earlier events of Sumerian civilization by the fantastical lengths of the reigns during the period before the Flood (Table 7.1). In addition, the King List does not even know about the period of more than 500 years when Uruk was dominant, *before* the first dynasty of Kish.

In fact, several scholars have argued that the ante-diluvian section of the King List was added as a 'prequel' about a hundred years after the main part of the King List was composed. The original version probably began after the Flood, with the descent of kingship from heaven at the foundation of the first dynasty of Kish. This would be appropriate because, as argued above, the office of kingship probably did originate at Kish. Before that time, political leadership was in the hands of the priesthood.

It has been suggested that the account of the ante-diluvial kings and the Flood was actually derived from the *Sumerian Flood Story*, a variant tradition on the Flood that shows some differences from the accounts in the *Gilgamesh* and *Atrahasis* epics. Hence, we can deduce that the Great Flood preceded the first dynasty of Kish, but we do not know by how much it preceded it. Since this is the most that we can safely deduce about the Flood from the King List, further progress in understanding the historical context of the Flood requires a search for physical remains of the Flood in the archaeological record of ancient Sumer. This search is critical for the understanding of Sumerian civilization, because the Flood was the pivotal event in their concept of history.

Excavation has revealed two physical records of major floods that predate the first dynasty of Kish. The more recent of the two is seen in the ancient city of Shuruppak, where an 'alluvial soil' possibly deposited by flood-waters was observed between the Proto-literate and Early Dynastic levels (ca. 3000 BC). As a candidate for the flood of Sumerian mythology, the flood deposit at Shuruppak is attractive, because in the *Gilgamesh Epic*, Shuruppak is stated to be the home of the Flood Hero. However, it is recognized that the flood event at Shuruppak did not markedly interrupt the continuity of Sumerian civilization. For example, there is no evidence whatever for a flood at this level in Uruk or Ur, which were already at this time great cities with monumental temple architecture. This is not consistent with the image of almost total annihilation depicted in both biblical and Mesopotamian Flood Stories, and therefore forces us to look for a more significant flood layer in the earlier record.

Such a deposit was found at Ur by Leonard Woolley, who carried out a major excavation over 60 feet (20 m) square and 60 feet deep to study this 'Flood Horizon' in detail. The excavation involved the removal of nearly 20,000 tons of soil, beginning at the level of a Royal Cemetery of Early Dynastic age, and reaching down to present day sea-level (Figure 7.4).

Below the cemetery, Woolley cut down through eight levels of house walls, the top five levels with plano-convex bricks laid in a herring-bone fashion, and the bottom three with flat bricks laid in the normal way. This transition in style of brick is recognized as a marker of the beginning of the Early Dynastic period, and was found at the 12 m level. Below the houses, Woolley encountered a vast deposit of broken pottery, totalling over 15 feet (5m) thick and containing pottery kilns at various levels. This was interpreted as an ancient vase factory. This factory must have operated over a prolonged period of time because the style of the pottery changed with depth through the section.

Below the pottery stratum, Woolley encountered a layer of water-lain silt over 10 feet (3 m) thick which he had previously seen in test pits . . . the Flood Horizon itself. Digging through the Flood Layer, Woolley again encountered pottery, with three successive floor levels, and finally, near present day sea-level, green clay pierced by brown root stains. This was interpreted as the virgin soil of a small island which must have risen slightly above the level of the surrounding marsh.

Based on the style of pottery fragments, the age of the Flood layer at Ur is dated to more than 4000 BC, and corresponds approximately to Level 6 at Eridu and Level 16 at Uruk (Figure 3.6). However, there is no evidence for any flood at this level in either of these other cities, respectively 20 km southwest and 60 km northwest of the city of Ur. Furthermore, Woolley suggested that even at Ur the whole city was not covered by the Flood Stratum, but only the side of the city nearest the river, which flowed next to the city at that time. Since again this does not fit the accounts of complete devastation in both Mesopotamian and biblical Flood Stories, we deduce that the most probable time for the Great Flood was before the foundation of Eridu, more than 5000 BC.

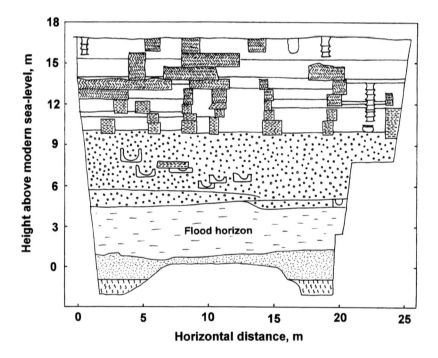

Figure 7.4. Cross section of Woolley's great Flood Pit at Ur, with heights relative to modern sea-level: 17 to 10 m = remains of walls; 10 to 5 m = pottery debris; 5 to 1 m = Flood deposit; +1 to -1 m = pre-Flood debris. Based on an excavation drawing by Woolley (1954).

Although there was never again a flood that threatened to wipe out all of human civilization, there must have been many large inundations during the 4th and 3rd millennia, given the susceptibility of the Mesopotamian plain to spring floods. Since there were no written records at this time, it seems probable that the Great Flood which gave rise to the Mesopotamian and biblical accounts became conflated with a more recent severe flood in the vicinity of ancient Shuruppak, around 3000 BC. Even this event occurred nearly 1000 years before the composition of the *Sumerian King List*, so it is easy to imagine how it could have been confused with the Great Flood 2000 years earlier.

Since there were no earlier records of royal succession, the original compilers of the King List began their account with the words:

> After the Flood,
> when kingship was lowered from heaven,
> the kingship was in Kish . . .
>
> [Translation: Jacobsen, 1939]

However, by implying that the Flood immediately preceded the kingdom of Kish, the King List appeared to bring the Flood 'forward' into human history, whereas it actually occurred in pre-history. The compilers of the King List probably had a sense that this was not correct, so to compensate for the shortness of the genealogical record, they attributed fantastically long reigns to the legendary kings of Kish, thereby pushing the Flood back into the remote past.

Chapter 8

The Flood as a geological event

If we place the Flood back in the prehistoric past, we must turn to geological evidence in order to constrain its time and place. Seven thousand years ago, when Eridu was founded, the Earth as well as the human race was in dramatic transition. The glaciers were in full retreat, following the end of the last Ice Age, and as they melted they released millions of cubic miles of water into the sea. Altogether, sea-level rose more than 330 feet (100 m) between 16,000 and 4000 years ago, causing huge changes in the Earth's landscape as once-dry valleys became flooded. This has led many people to wonder if there was any connection between sea-level rise and the story of the Flood in biblical and Mesopotamian literature.

With a present-day water depth of less than 300 feet, the Persian Gulf was a dry valley during the last Ice Age. As the glaciers melted, the sea would have advanced up the Gulf at a rate of a few hundred feet per year. This advance of the sea could hardly have given rise to the story of a great flood. However, if the sea was held back for a while by a natural rock dam, it would have released a flood of water when sea-level flooded over the top of the dam.

There are no great natural dams in the floor of the Persian Gulf, but there is such a submerged dam between the Mediterranean and the Black Sea, about 1000 miles from Mesopotamia. This natural dam consists of the Bosporus Strait, which is only about 100 feet (30 m) deep, and which separates the Black Sea from the Sea of Marmora. The latter is itself connected to the Mediterranean via the Dardanelles Strait, which has a depth of about 250 feet (Figure 8.1). In a book published in 1998, William Ryan and Walter Pitman suggested that when rising sea level over-topped the Bosporus dam, it would have caused sudden flooding of the Black Sea basin, thus giving rise to the biblical and Mesopotamian flood stories.

At the present day, the level of the Black Sea is about one foot (30 cm) higher than the Sea of Marmora, due to the rivers that empty into the Black Sea from Eastern Europe. This difference in water-level leads to a net outflow from the Black Sea to the Mediterranean. The large influx of river water also makes the Black Sea less salty than the Mediterranean, and this less salty water 'floats' on the surface of the sea as it flows out to the Mediterranean. However, the dense salty waters in the Mediterranean push in the opposite direction near the sea floor, creating a smaller

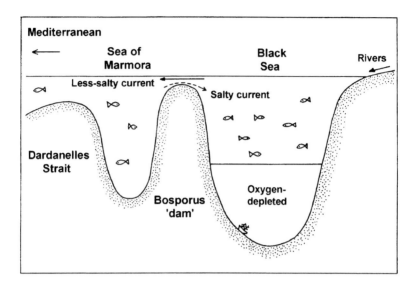

Figure 8.1. Schematic cross section between the Black Sea and Mediterranean showing water currents through the Bosporus Strait at the present day. (Vertical exaggeration ca. 1000 times)

inward flow of salty water along the bottom of the Bosporus Strait (Figure 8.1). Because this water is denser than the surface water of the Black Sea, the two types of water do not completely mix, and a separate layer of dense salty water exists at the bottom of the Black Sea. This bottom layer is also depleted in oxygen, so that it acts like a 'time capsule' to preserve ancient wooden artifacts such as shipwrecks.

We know that the Mediterranean dropped below the level of the Dandanelles and Bosporus straights during the last Ice age, and that it would have over-topped these dams when sea-level rose again. However, the question of whether this would cause a massive flood depends on what level of water existed in the Black Sea at the time when the Bosporus dam was breached. Ryan and Pitman suggested that the level of the Black Sea fell dramatically around 8000 BC, due to a drop in the amount of rainfall in Eastern Europe. With its supply of water cut off, the water level would have fallen due to evaporation, causing the level of the Black Sea to drop as much as 500 feet (150 m) below its present-day level. Hence, they suggested that when rising sea-level over-topped the Bosporus dam around 6000 BC, it would have created a giant waterfall with 200 times the power of Niagara Falls (Figure 8.2a). The resulting rise in the level of the Black Sea (a few inches per day) would have flooded communities living on the shore of the ancient sea. Ryan and Pitman suggested that these people fled to other regions of the Middle East, carrying orally-transmitted accounts of a great flood that gave rise to the biblical and Sumerian flood stories.

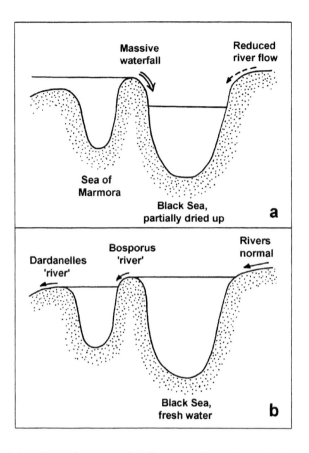

Figure 8.2. Alternative scenarios for water flow through the Bosporus around 6000 BC. a) Model of Ryan and Pitman, assuming the Black Sea partially dried up. b) Model of Aksu and co-workers (2002), assuming European rainfall similar to the present-day.

Other geologists studying the evolution of the Black Sea since the time of the last Ice Age have come to different conclusions. For example, Ali Aksu and co-workers argue that there has been an outflow of fresh water from the Black Sea for most of the last 16,000 years, leading to a waterfall in the opposite direction (Figure 8.2b). When sea-level rose above the Bosporus 'dam', this waterfall would have turned into the outward water current from the Black Sea that is observed at the present day. However, as the level of the Mediterranean continued to rise, the increasing pressure of its dense salty water finally set up a flow in the opposite direction along the bottom of the Bosporus Strait.

To evaluate Ryan and Pitman's theory of a Black Sea Flood, we must look at it on two different levels, geological and literary. Geological evidence in favour of the Flood theory was provided by Ryan and Pitman's discovery of what appeared to be an ancient beach, 350 feet below the present level of the Black Sea, which they interpreted as the shore-line of the 'Black Sea lake' immediately before the Flood. Fossils from this beach, recovered by dredging, gave calibrated radiocarbon ages around 5500 BC. To further investigate this deposit, the underwater explorer Robert Ballard led an expedition to the Black Sea, using side scan sonar and a remotely operated diving vehicle (ROV) to examine the beach and its shore-line. The search revealed scattered blocks of stone and timber about 300 feet below the present sea surface. These appeared to be the remains of a Neolithic settlement established on the shore of the ancient Black Sea, before the Flood (Figure 8.3). However, radiocarbon dating of the timbers revealed that they were all less than 300 years old, so the interpretation as a Neolithic settlement is unlikely.

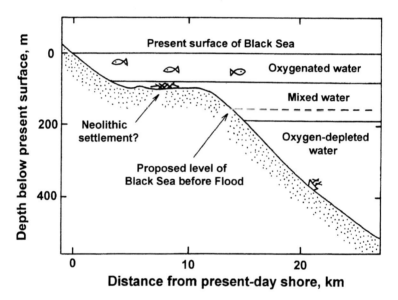

Figure 8.3. Cross section of the Black Sea showing a proposed Neolithic settlement near an ancient beach. Based on Ballard *et al.* (2001).

Geological evidence against the Flood theory was summarized in a special issue of the journal *Marine Geology* in October 2002. One of the most important observations was the existence of a delta at the southern end of the Bosporus Strait, which must have been formed by water flowing *out* of the Black Sea. Radiocarbon dates indicate that the delta was deposited between 8000 and 7000 BC, thus providing strong evidence that there was an outflow of water from the Black Sea at this time, shortly before the proposed date of the Black Sea Flood. However, Ryan and his co-workers countered that the level of the Black Sea could have fallen even more sharply, after 7000 BC.

Although the geological evidence for or against the Black Sea Flood is not conclusive, the literary evidence is decisive. Firstly, both the *Gilgamesh Epic* and Genesis speak of the annihilation of the whole population, except for the inhabitants of the Ark; whereas the Black Sea Flood would have been so gradual that the population could easily have escaped. Secondly, and even more conclusively, the Flood described in Genesis and the *Gilgamesh Epic* eventually dried up, whereas the 'flood' waters of the Black Sea never went down. Hence, we must conclude that the literary stories of the Flood are based on a seasonal river flood, and are completely unrelated to any events that occurred at the Black Sea. Instead, these stories perfectly describe the devastating floods of the Mesopotamian plain, which have even been experienced in the recent historical past.

The land of Mesopotamia is one of the largest flood plains on Earth, with a slope of less than one in ten thousand from Baghdad to the Gulf Coast. Hence it has always been susceptible to flooding in springtime, when melt waters from mountain snows in the north swell the Tigris and Euphrates rivers. Furthermore, the deposition of sediment by these rivers tends to make them flow in beds that are actually elevated above the surrounding plain (Figure 8.4). This elevated configuration of the rivers lent itself ideally to ancient agriculture, since water could be drawn off in canals to irrigate the land (technically a delta plain). However, if the rivers burst the levees that form their banks, thousands of square miles can be flooded in an instant, and the water will remain on the land for weeks or months before it can drain away.

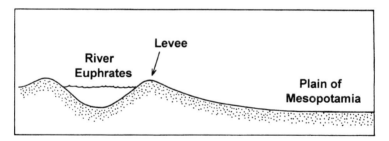

Figure 8.4. Schematic cross section of the River Euphrates showing the elevation of the river bed above the surrounding delta plain (not to scale).

Although widespread flooding was a regular occurrence in Iraq until the recent construction of major dams, environmental evidence suggests that a wet climatic period between 7000 BC and 5500 BC would have caused even more devastating floods during that period. One source of evidence for this wet period comes from a cave site near Jerusalem, in which stalactites provide a record of past climatic conditions. This record was created when successive layers of lime were deposited on the stalactites, over a period of thousands of years, by dripping groundwater. Analysis of the layered structure of one stalactite revealed two periods of extensive local flooding in the last 10,000 years, indicated by large perturbations in the stable

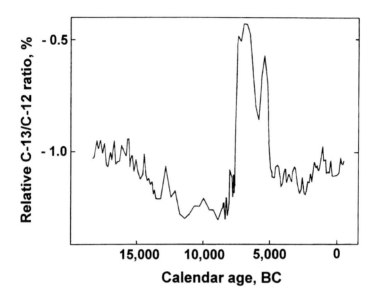

Figure 8.5. Carbon isotope record from a cave stalactite near Jerusalem, indicating two periods of frequent local flooding, around 7000 and 5500 BC. Based on Bar-Matthews *et al.* (1997, 2000).

carbon isotope composition of water entering the cave system. Dating of these periods of flooding by the uranium-thorium isotope method showed that they peaked at around 7000 and 5500 BC (Figure 8.5).

The evidence from the Jerusalem cave is indicative of climatic conditions in the Eastern Mediterranean, at the western end of the fertile crescent. However, even more pertinent evidence for the flood history of the Tigris and Euphrates comes from Lake Van, a self-contained drainage basin in southeast Turkey that lies between the headwaters of these two rivers (see Figure 1.1).

Lake Van is an example of a 'Terminal Lake', which is fed by rivers but has no outflow. The levels of such lakes are determined by a balance between water input from rivers and water loss by evaporation, and they are therefore very useful as monitors of past climate. During wet periods the lake level rises, whereas in dry periods the lake level falls and salinity increases to the point where salt deposits may form (as seen around the Dead Sea). The level of Lake Van varies by about two feet on a seasonal basis, with a marked rise in May from a combination of snow melt and spring rain, followed by a drop over the summer due to enhanced evaporation. Variations of over four feet in lake level also occur between wet and dry years. However, sediment deposits on the floor of the lake record changes in lake level of over 1300 feet (400 m) over the past 14,000 years (Figure 8.6). These deposits can be precisely dated because the bottom sediments of Lake Van show annual bands called varves, which can be counted to determine their age.

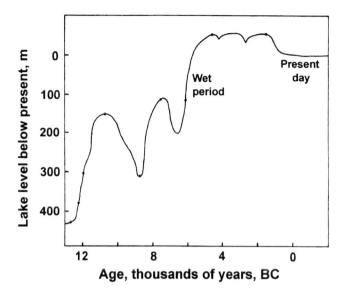

Figure 8.6. Reconstruction of water level fluctuations in Lake Van from the end of the last Ice Age to the present day. Based on Landmann *et al.* (1996).

Past variations in the water-level of Lake Van are summarized in Figure 8.6 for the period from the present to 12,000 BC. This diagram shows three periods when lake level rose very sharply, corresponding to periods of prolonged wet conditions. However, because the underwater shape of the lake is like an inverted cone, its volume increases markedly as the water level rises. Therefore, the most recent increase in lake volume must have been substantially larger than the previous two. To evaluate these effects more critically, the data from Figure 8.6 were combined with estimates of the under-water shape of the lake in order to estimate the history of water influx into the lake. The results are shown in Figure 8.7, corrected for surface evaporation. This diagram shows that the period around 6000 BC was by far the wettest since the end of the Ice Age, with rainfall nearly four times greater than the present day. Since Lake Van lies near the headwaters of the Tigris and Euphrates, the peak at 6000 BC truly represents the 'smoking gun' of the Great Flood.

Based on a combination of the evidence from Lake Van, the Jerusalem stalactite, and archaeological remains from Mesopotamia, we can now attempt to reconstruct the approximate settlement history of ancient Sumer. This history begins on the upper reaches of the Euphrates (eastern Syria and southern Turkey) where the Agricultural Revolution took place. Here, in Neolithic settlements such as Abu Hureyra, we find evidence for a transition from hunting and gathering to cereal cultivation and animal husbandry, which occurred between 9000 and 7000 BC.

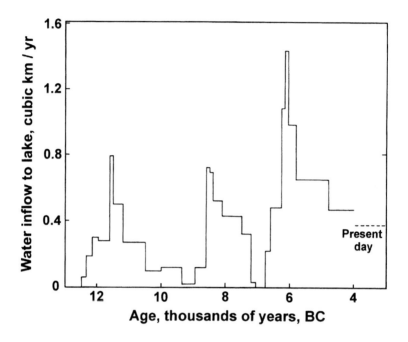

Figure 8.7. Reconstruction of past water influx into Lake Van, indicating extremely wet conditions around 6000 BC. Based on data from Figure 8.6.

At the present day, Abu Hureyra lies at the southerly edge of the Fertile Crescent (Figure 8.8), where annual rainfall of greater than 10 inches (25 cm) per year permits cereal farming without the need for irrigation ('dry farming'). Further to the south, on the plains of Mesopotamia, farming has only been possible in historical times with the aid of irrigation. However, the first of the wet periods recorded in the Jerusalem cave (around 7000 BC) probably extended the fertile crescent into Mesopotamia. This would have encouraged farmers to move eastward from their earlier settlements on the upper reaches of the Euphrates, to settle on the fertile plains of southern Mesopotamia.

This situation changed around 6500 BC, as a drying of the climate returned rainfall patterns to something like the present day. This probably forced farmers to move into close proximity with the Euphrates, in order to farm the river-banks that were kept moist by ground-water. However, the tendency for settlements to cluster near the river would have increased the risk of flood damage, so that when wet conditions returned around 6000 BC, all the settlements of the plain were on low-lying land susceptible to flooding. Hence, when paleo-climatic evidence is combined with the archaeological evidence from Mesopotamian cities, it seems most likely that the Great Flood occurred between 6000 and 5500 BC, shortly before the founding of Eridu.

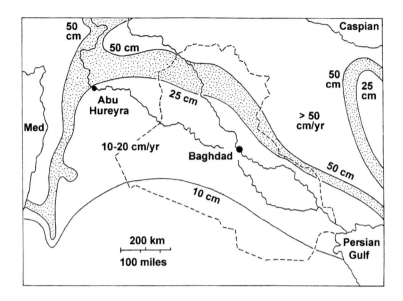

Figure 8.8. Distribution of rainfall over the Middle East at the present day. Abu Hureyra is an example of a Neolithic settlement that grew up within the limit of dry farming (annual rainfall around 10 inches per year).

Chapter 9

Religion before the Flood

If we try to look back 'before the Flood' to see what religious life was like in the earliest period of human culture, we are beyond the range of archaeological remains on the southern Mesopotamian plain. To the north, we find many small settlements going back to the period of the agricultural revolution around 7000 BC. However, the most important archaeological evidence for the origin of religion is a type of sculpture that actually goes back much further than the origins of agriculture, perhaps to the first arrival of modern humans in Europe and the Middle East from Africa.

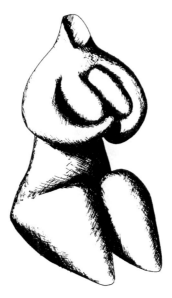

Figure 9.1. Female figurine from Northern Mesopotamia interpreted as an embodiment of the numinous power of fertility. Height 7 cm. British Museum.

This type of sculpture is a model of the human female form with features that draw attention to her motherhood. For example, Figure 9.1 shows a clay model from Northern Mesopotamia that has prominent breasts. This example dates to about 6000 BC; however, similar examples are scattered widely over Europe and the Middle East, dating as far back as 26,000 BC. These sculptures have often been described as Venus (= Ishtar/Inanna). However, this is a misnomer, because in Mesopotamian mythology, Ishtar/Inanna is the goddess of sexual love, but is never a mother. In fact, Inanna's roots go back to her role as the goddess of the temple storehouse, whereas figures like the one illustrated here are thought to be forerunners of the Mother Goddess (named either Nintur or Ninhursaga in the Sumerian pantheon).

An older example of this type of figure, dating to around 20,000 BC, was carved into a cave wall in the Dordogne region of France (Figure 9.2). She holds one hand on her belly, as if to highlight a pregnancy, and in the other she holds a bison horn with 13 notches cut into it. It is widely believed that these notches represent the days for the new moon to grow full, which therefore links the cycle of female fertility to the phases of the moon. One puzzling feature of this carving is the head, which appears to be beaked like a bird; however, the example in Figure 9.1 lacks any head at all, as is commonly the case with these figures. Leaving aside the question of the head, these figurines suggest a reverence for the mystical power of motherhood, which is one example of the many mystical powers which are seen in nature.

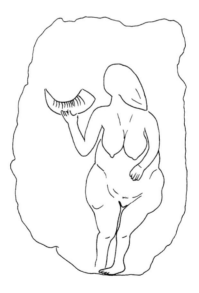

Figure 9.2. Carved wall relief from a cave in southern France. ca. 20-25,000 BC (43 cm high, limestone). Aquitaine Museum, Bordeaux, France.

In his classic book, *The Idea of the Holy*, Rudolph Otto called these mystical powers of nature *numina*. The idea of the Holy arises from mankind's recognition that these numinous powers are beyond human understanding, and must therefore be separated from the profane matters of everyday human existence. This separation is fundamental to the concept of holiness, and is very well illustrated by Israelite religious laws, recorded in the biblical book of Exodus.

After the Israelites escaped from Egypt, they fled across the desert until they reached the prominent peak of Mount Sinai. Here the whole community had a profound religious experience, in which the presence of God was manifested on the top of the mountain in the form of an earthquake, a violently thundering cloud, and a deafening trumpet blast. The Israelites were forbidden even to touch the bottom of the sacred mountain, on pain of death.

Following God's appearance on the mountain, a special tent called the 'Tabernacle' was established as a sacred place that was devoted to God *within* the Israelite camp. The presence of God in the Most Holy Place of the Tabernacle was represented by a glowing cloud that hovered over the sacred 'Ark of the Covenant', and several barriers were established between this sacred space and the profane space of human habitation (Figure 9.3).

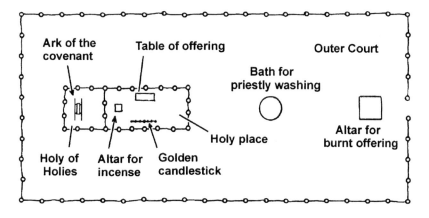

Figure 9.3. Plan of the Tabernacle, showing successive barriers between the Holy and profane, based on the instructions given in the book of Exodus.

The outermost space of the Tabernacle was the courtyard, which contained an altar for burnt offering. This was separated from the camp, but the common people were permitted to enter. The next space was the Holy Place, which contained an altar for incense. Only the priests were allowed to enter this space, and only after they had been ceremonially washed. Finally, there was the Most Holy Place, which contained the Ark of the Covenant. Only the High Priest was allowed to enter this space, and only after he had been smeared with the blood of an animal sacrifice.

When the sons of the High Priest broke these taboos by making an 'unauthorized' incense offering before the Lord, they were themselves consumed by fire (Leviticus, Ch 10).

An examination of Sumerian literature by Emily Wilson showed that thousands of years before the Tabernacle of the Israelites, the Sumerians had a similar concept of the holiness of their temples as places that were the realm of the gods. This is shown by the distinction between the Sumerian word 'holy' (*ku*) and the word 'pure' (*sikil*) which means 'ritually clean' but does not directly imply the presence of God. *Sikil* is used where the sense is to purify a person or an object in order to present them to the gods, but only *ku* is used of the dwelling of the gods themselves. On the other hand, the equivalent Akkadian word (*ellu*) has a much more general meaning which includes the Sumerian *ku* (holy), but can also mean simply that something is clean, such as clean laundry.

Wilson concluded from a detailed study of the use of these words that, prior to their encounter with the Sumerians, the Semitic peoples of Mesopotamia did not have a clear concept of holiness, in the sense of the unapproachability of the gods. Instead, it appears that early Akkadian religion was mainly focussed on purification from uncleanness (evil spirits). Therefore, we can conclude that the immanence of divine power in the Holy Place was first experienced by the Sumerians, rather than the Semitic peoples who lived round about them.

Figure 9.4. Depiction of the Mother goddess with new-born babies. The curled objects are thought to represent umbilical cords, and are her most common symbol. From a clay plaque of the Old Babylonian period. 12 cm high. Musée du Louvre.

It has been suggested that in the Neolithic period (beginning at 10,000 BC) the numinous power of female fertility began to be personified as the Mother Goddess (Figure 9.4). In contrast, the origin of the Cosmic Triad (which dominated later Sumerian religion) remains a mystery. However, we can get our clearest understanding of the relationship between the Mother Goddess and the Cosmic Triad by examining the Flood Story. Not only is this preserved in three different Mesopotamian versions, but there is clear evidence that these share a common source with the biblical Flood Story. The three Mesopotamian versions of the Flood Story have survived in different degrees of completeness, but important sections are present in all three versions which allow the identities of the principle gods and goddesses to be compared.

In the *Sumerian Flood Story*, four deities, listed in the order Anu, Enlil, Enki, and Ninhursaga, are all involved in the creation of the Sumerian people (i.e. mankind). Of these four, the goddess Ninhursaga is the most shadowy figure. Her name means 'Lady of the foothills' (nin-hursag), referring to the lands on the norther border of the Mesopotamian plain, but she seems to have been a primaeval Mother Goddess. Her name may indicate that she was not originally a goddess of Sumer, but was brought to Mesopotamia by the nomadic peoples who lived in the northern steppes. Following the creation of mankind in the Flood Story, it is Ninhursaga who allots the first Sumerian cities to their divine patrons (based on the translation by Jacobsen, 1987). This allotment begins with the dedication of Eridu to Enki, but does not mention either Uruk or Nippur (devoted to Anu and Enlil).

In contrast to her major role in the *Sumerian Flood Story*, Ninhursaga is not even mentioned in the Flood Story of the Akkadian epics, where the Cosmic Triad stand alone as the supreme gods. However, the Mother Goddess is represented in another of her guises in all three Mesopotamian accounts of the Flood. This is as Nintur, the mother of the human race, who grieves for the destruction of mankind in the Flood, but is helpless to intervene. The goddesses Ninhursaga and Nintur are both believed to be manifestations of the Mother Goddess, although the relationship between them is very unclear. Nevertheless, it seems that the muddled picture here is of the diminishing importance of the primaeval Mother Goddess through time.

When we look at the divine names used in the Genesis Flood Story, we find two alternative names for God used in different parts of the account. This led to the theory that the Israelites originally had two written documents describing the Flood (each of which used a different word for God), which were subsequently combined into the single complete account we have today. Hence, this theory is usually referred to as the 'Documentary Hypothesis'. Figure 9.5 illustrates the way in which the two hypothetical source documents are supposed to have been interleaved to make the complete account. The 'Yahwist' document (J) is so named because it uses the divine name of Yahweh (= Jehovah) whereas the 'Priestly' document (P) uses the divine name Elohim.

If the Documentary Hypothesis were correct, we might expect to see some evidence for two distinct sources in the Mesopotamian accounts of the Flood. However, when we compare the biblical and Mesopotamian accounts in detail, we

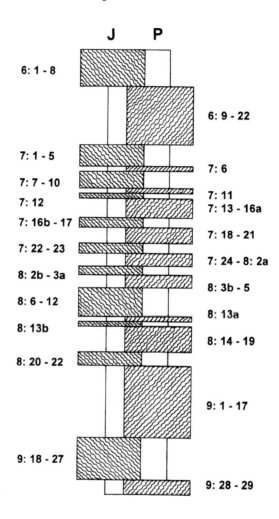

Figure 9.5. Application of the Documentary Hypothesis to the biblical
Flood Story, showing the proposed interleaving of the hypothetical source
documents J and P. Based on Blenkinsopp (1985).

find that the Mesopotamian versions of the story have more similarities with the
'complete account' in Genesis than either of the hypothetical sources required by
the Documentary Hypothesis. This is shown in Table 9.1 by the fact that both the
'J' and 'P' accounts together are required to incorporate all the details of the story
found in the Mesopotamian sources (of which the *Gilgamesh Epic* is the most
complete). This suggests that the hypothetical sources 'J' and 'P' never actually
existed in the Flood Story, but that the complete biblical account shares a common
source with the Mesopotamian versions.

Table 9.1. Comparison of specific episodes in the biblical Flood Story attributed to the hypothetical sources 'J' and 'P', with the same episodes in the Mesopotamian accounts. 'Y' = material is present: 'N' = not; '?' = unknown (missing section).

Event in the story	Genesis Source#	Mesopotamian* G	A	S
1. The Flood was caused by divine plan.	J	Y	Y	?
2. A reason is given for the Flood.	P&J	N	Y	?
2. The hero was warned by divine revelation.	P	Y	Y	Y
3. Hero instructed to build a large boat of a given size.	P	Y	Y	?
4. The hero is attentive and obeys the divine command.	P&J	Y	Y	?
5. Animals as well as people were loaded on the boat.	P&J	Y	Y	?
6. The hero was instructed to enter the boat.	J	Y	N	?
7. The door was closed.	J	Y	Y	?
8. Duration of rain and flood-water rise is described.	P&J	Y	Y	Y
9. The death of mankind is described.	P&J	Y	Y	N
10. The end of the rain is described.	P&J	Y	?	Y
11. The grounding on a mountain is described.	P	Y	?	N
12. The hero opens a window.	J	Y	?	Y
13 Duration of waiting for waters to subside is described.	J	Y	?	N
14. Hero sends out birds to test for abating of the Flood.	J	Y	?	N
15. Hero offers sacrifices of worship after he is delivered.	J	Y	Y	Y
16. Divine appreciation of the sacrfice is described.	J	Y	Y	?
17. The hero receives a divine blessing.	P	Y	?	Y

Biblical sources: J =Yahwist, P = Priestly source. * Mesopotamian sources: G = *Gilgamesh Epic*; A = *Atrahasis Epic*; S = *Sumerian Flood Story*. Modified after Wenham (1978, 1987).

If the biblical Flood Story was derived as a complete entity from an earlier Mesopotamian source, this raises the question of why it uses two divine names, Elohim and Yahweh, in the place of the three divine names of the Cosmic Triad. There is no simple answer to this question, but it probably arose during the long process of transmission from an original Sumerian version to the final Hebrew version. During this process, it was necessary to translate the divine names, since the Cosmic Triad was unknown to the Hebrews. For example, by the time the Flood Story was being translated into Hebrew, the star sign that originally represented the God of Heaven had become a generic name for any god. Therefore, it would have been appropriate to translate this name as 'Elohim', the generic Hebrew divine name, just as 'God' is in English. On the other hand, both En-lil and En-ki are specific divine names with the same prefix (En = Lord), so it would have been appropriate to translate both of these as 'Yahweh', which is also translated as 'Lord' in English. Hence, three divine names could have become two.

This raises the question of what happened to the Mother Goddess who appears in the Mesopotamian versions of the Flood Story. To answer this question, we must understand the significance of the Sumerian cult of 'Sacred Marriage' between the gods, which was discussed earlier. According to this doctrine, most of the great gods had consorts who were regarded as their wives, and the temple contained a marriage bed to permit their sexual union. This doctrine was acted out in the Rite of Sacred Marriage, when the High Priest (impersonating the god) slept with a Priestess (impersonating the goddess, his consort) in the marriage bed of the god.

Evidence for the early establishment of this Sumerian ritual comes from an archaic cylinder seal (Figure 9.6), found in the layers below the Early Dynastic royal tombs at Ur. The lower panel of this seal shows a woman standing next to a temple and holding the ringed pole which is the symbol of the goddess Inanna. However, the upper panel shows a couple engaged in lovemaking, whose close association with the temple points to it as a depiction of the rite of Sacred Marriage.

Figure 9.6. Seal impression from Ur showing evidence for ritual sex. British Museum.

Further evidence for this interpretation comes from the *Hymn to Kesh*, which is one of the very earliest Sumerian Temple Hymns, known from the dawn of Sumerian literature in the Early Dynastic period. Only a few fragments remain of the Early Dynastic version, but these are sufficient to show that the hymn was accurately reproduced for 1000 years until the Old Babylonian period. Based on these Old Babylonian versions of the Hymn, it is clear that the Temple of Kesh was devoted to the Mother Goddess, Nintur. However, the critical passage describing the Rite of Sacred Marriage is found in lines 103-104:

The holy house of Kesh, the extravagant provider of which is the bedroom
The house– its En-priests are Anunnaki gods

[Translation: Jacobsen, 1987]

Here, we can see that the chief priests (En-priests) impersonated the heavenly gods (Anunnaki = children of Anu) in the rite of Sacred Marriage with the priestesses of the Mother Goddess.

Later in Sumerian history, when kingship eclipsed the priesthood in importance, the role of the god in the rite of sacred marriage was acted by the king, and the role of the Mother Goddess was replaced by Inanna (*Ishtar*), Queen of Heaven. Indeed, a poem called the *Hymn to Inanna* describes just such a union between King Iddin-Dagan (of the Isin dynasty) and a priestess representing the goddess Inanna. Gilgamesh, King of Uruk, was himself probably conceived in this type of ritual, since the *Gilgamesh Epic* attributes his parentage to King Lugal-banda and the goddess Ninsun. He was consequently said to be two-thirds divine and one third mortal.

Gilgamesh was the archetypal hero of ancient mythology (Figure 9.7), and probably inspired many of the heroic characters of later cultures, including those of Assyria, Persia, Greece and Rome. Therefore, the writer of Genesis was probably thinking of Gilgamesh when he wrote the introduction to the biblical Flood Story (Gen 6:4):

The Nephilim were on the earth in those days–and also afterward–when the sons of God went to the daughters of men and had children by them. They were the heroes of old, men of renown.

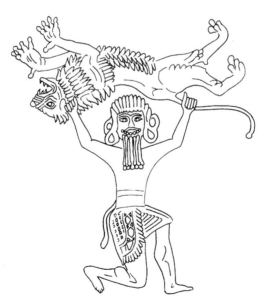

Figure 9.7. Depiction of a hero wrestling with a lion, probably based on the figure of Gilgamesh. From an Assyrian cylinder seal, ca. 1200 BC. British Museum.

The 'sons of god' described in this verse were the 'Anunnaki', or sons of the heavenly god Anu. Hence, this suggests that in performing the rite of Sacred Marriage, the high priests were impersonating the Anunnaki, and thus claiming to be the Sons of God. This interpretation is supported by the *Sumerian King List*, which describes Gilgamesh as the son of a high priest of Kulab (one of the principal temples of Uruk). However, the King List also refers to this High Priest in a more sinister way as a 'lillu demon'. So it is not surprising that immediately after describing the parentage of the heroes, the Genesis text condemns the sinfulness of mankind (Gen 6:5&7):

> The LORD saw how great man's wickedness on the earth had become, and that every inclination of the thoughts of his heart was only evil all the time . . . So the LORD said, "I will wipe mankind, whom I have created, from the face of the earth, . . . for I am grieved that I have made them."

Therefore, it was evidently the involvement of the priesthood in the rite of Sacred Marriage with the priestesses of the Mother Goddess that was identified in Genesis as the sin which provoked the judgement of the Flood. Thus, the involvement of the Mother Goddess in the religion of ancient Sumer was the main point of contention between the Mesopotamian and biblical authors. The former saw the Mother Goddess as equal to the Cosmic Triad in importance, whereas the latter saw the mixing of the cult of the Mother Goddess with the cult of the Cosmic Triad as the perversion that led to the Flood.

This focus in Genesis on the corruption of the temple cult can also explain the strange description of the flooding of the Mountains in the biblical Flood Story (Gen 7:17-20):

> For forty days the flood kept coming on the earth, and as the waters increased they lifted the ark high above the earth. . . . They rose greatly on the earth and all the high mountains under the entire heavens were covered. The waters rose more than twenty feet, and the mountains were covered.

The description of the waters covering '*all the high mountains under the entire heavens*' has caused much consternation, and led biblical fundamentalists to infer that the Flood covered the whole globe. However, this verse must actually be referring to the temples of ancient Sumer, which were built on *artificial* mountains. For example, the temple at Nippur was called the *E-kur* or 'House of the Mountain', and temples in other Sumerian cities were referred to in similar ways. This temple on top of the mountain was the site of the cultic marriage bed of the god. Therefore, when these temple mountains were all covered by the Flood, it must have seemed to the survivors on the Ark as if the Earth had been 'wiped clean by the wrath of God'.

Obviously there are no surviving records of the nature of the sacred mountains built before the Flood, since only the Flood Hero survived the deluge. However,

Figure 9.8. Impression of an Akkadian cylinder seal showing the Sun god rising from behind artificial mountains. British Museum.

there are pictorial records of 'sacred mountains' in later Mesopotamian art, one of the best examples being an Akkadian cylinder seal from ca. 2300 BC (Figure 9.8). This shows a mythological scene in which the Sun god rises over what appears to be a square-cornered artificial mountain. The Sun god is identified by the rays coming from his shoulders, and by the serrated knife which he uses to cut a hole in the earth as he rises each morning.

The temple mountain shown in Figure 9.8 was probably built of kiln-fired bricks, a technique that has allowed the ziggurats of the Third Millennium BC to survive, partially intact, even up to the present day. In contrast, the early temple platforms were built only of sun-dried bricks, so that the waters of the Flood must have had a devastating effect on them, reducing them to mere 'mountains of mud'.

When the ark grounded on the mountains of Aratta (Ararat) on the eastern edge of the plains of Mesopotamia, we can imagine that the Flood hero must have looked westwards across the retreating floodwaters and seen a completely empty landscape. Much later, cults dedicated to the Mother goddess probably diffused back into Mesopotamia from the peoples who lived in the northern foothills. However, these cults of Ninhursaga never again rose to the same prominence that they had once held, so the worship of the Cosmic Triad became the central feature of the religion of the Sumerians, even up until the time of Abraham.

Chapter 10

Stories of Creation and Paradise

In the last chapter we compared the Mesopotamian and biblical Flood stories and saw how they must have come from a common Sumerian source. We might also expect to see commonality between the Mesopotamian and biblical Creation stories, but here the picture is more complex.

The Mesopotamian work that has most often been compared with the opening chapters of Genesis is the Babylonian creation epic, *Enuma Elish*. There are indeed parallels between Genesis and *Enuma Elish*: both works begin with a watery chaos, and both describe the divine act of separating the Heavens and the Earth. However, in *Enuma Elish* tablet 4, this act involves the gruesome butchery of the sea goddess Tiamat, and has little in common with the simplicity and directness of the Genesis account of separation. This contrast is not surprising, because the Babylonian creation epic is a 'revisionist' work mainly concerned with the elevation of Marduk above the other gods of the Mesopotamian pantheon. It therefore presents only a garbled version of earlier Sumerian mythology.

If we go directly to Sumerian myths of creation, we find stronger parallels with Genesis, but many of these stories also seem to be badly corrupted. For example, in several Sumerian myths, even the great gods Enlil and Enki have been portrayed as adulterous womanizers. This might lead us to give up altogether on the search for Sumerian parallels to the biblical account of creation, but this would be a mistake, because remnants of material common with Genesis are still present in these myths.

One of the most difficult aspects of Sumerian mythology is the tendency for different creation accounts to be associated with the different cult centres. But even in Genesis, we see two creation accounts (Ch1 and Ch2) with very different cosmological viewpoints. Significantly, these different viewpoints find parallels in the creation stories associated with the major cult centres of Nippur and Eridu.

A major theme of the cosmology of Nippur was separation. For example, two Sumerian myths, *Gilgamesh, Enkidu and the underworld* and *The creation of the pick-axe* both begin by describing the separation of the Heavens and the Earth, after which Enlil's temple at Nippur became the 'bond between Heaven and Earth'. These accounts bear more comparison with the Genesis account of separation than the macabre story in *Enuma Elish*:

After Heaven had been moved away from Earth
After Earth had been separated from Heaven
After the name of man had been fixed . . .

The Lord whose decisions are unalterable,
Enlil, who brings up the seed of the land from the earth,
Took care to move away Heaven from Earth,
Took care to move away Earth from Heaven.

[Translations: Kramer, 1944]

The corresponding account in Genesis is found in Chapter 1, verses 6-8:

And God said, "Let there be an expanse between the waters to separate water from
water." So God made the expanse and separated the water under the expanse from
the water above it.

A further similarity between Genesis and Nippur theology is the description of the
Spirit of God hovering over the chaotic waters in Genesis 1:2:

Now the earth was formless and empty, darkness was over the surface of the deep,
and the Spirit of God was hovering over the waters.

The word used here for the Spirit of God is actually the 'Wind' of God, which
corresponds to the 'lil' of Enlil, meaning something like a gentle wind or breath (i.e.
the 'Breath of God').

There are even stronger parallels between 'Eridu theology' and Genesis 2.
Thus, according to Genesis Chapter 2, when the Lord God made Adam, he placed
him in a garden in Eden (Gen 2:8). *Edin* is the Sumerian word for a plain, and the
next verses state that the Garden was watered by a river with four tributaries, two
of which were the Tigris and Euphrates. Hence, the biblical account places the
creation of mankind in the Land between the Rivers, or the plain of Mesopotamia.

Sumerian mythology also describes the creation of mankind by the Lord of the
Earth (Enki). He is the god of fresh (living) waters, and is often identified in
Sumerian art (Figure 10.1) by the fact that he holds a vase in each hand, from which
fountains well up to supply streams of water. The life-giving character of these
waters is sometimes indicated by fish swimming in their overflowing streams.

The impression in Figure 10.1 was made from a cylinder seal dating to around
2300 BC. It shows an 'introduction scene', which is a common theme for seals of
that period. The owner of the seal is shown in the middle of the scene, with the
shaven head and bordered gown that was typical of Sumerian attire. The other three
figures in the scene are all gods, as indicated by their horned head-dresses. In the
centre of the scene, a 'family god' grasps the left hand of the worshipper and
introduces him to the great god, Enki, seated at right on his throne. The two flowing
vases held by Enki represent the great rivers, Tigris and Euphrates, while the other

Figure 10.1. Impression of an Akkadian cylinder seal showing Enki as the god of living waters. Musée du Louvre.

flowing vases under his throne represent what the Bible calls the 'springs of the great deep' (Gen 7:11). In Genesis Chapter 2, these springs are said to water the surface of the ground (v. 6), because the Lord God had not sent any rain on the land. The Great Deep was called the Apsu by the Sumerians, and was conceived of as a huge reservoir of underground fresh water, on which Enki's temple was founded at Eridu (Figure 10.2).

We can see from these comparisons that an emphasis on the importance of water is found in both the Genesis 2 and Eridu creation traditions. In addition, a second similarity between them is seen in the account of the creation of mankind. According to another Sumerian myth, Enki made mankind from the clay of the Apsu, displaying a remarkable parallel with the account in Genesis 2:7:

> The Lord God formed the man (Adam) from the dust of the ground and breathed into his nostrils the breath of life, and he became a living being.

The creation of mankind by Enki is described in more detail in the *Atrahasis Epic*. After mixing clay with the blood of a slaughtered god, the Mother Goddess, under Enki's supervision, pinches off fourteen pieces of clay to make seven males and seven females. These are then placed into the womb goddess, and after nine months the offspring of the gods come forth to found the human race:

> Geshtu-e, a god who had intelligence, they slaughtered in their assembly
> Nintu mixed clay with his flesh and blood
> They heard the drumbeat (heartbeat) for ever after
> A ghost came into existence from the god's flesh
> And she (the Mother Goddess) proclaimed it as his living sign.
>
> [Translation: Dalley, 1989]

Figure 10.2. Cylinder seal impression showing the Sea House of Enki, floating on the waters of the Apsu. University Museum, Pennsylvania.

Of course, there are also differences between the *Atrahasis Epic* and the Genesis creation story. For example, in the epic, the reason for man's creation is to save the gods from the drudgery of manual labour involved in agriculture. Henceforth, mankind would clean the irrigation ditches, plant and harvest crops, tend the livestock, and present the fruits of all this labour to the gods in their temples. The food that was presented in the temples was regarded very tangibly as the gods' sustenance, and if the presentation of food and drink offerings was interrupted (as occurred during the Flood in the *Atrahasis Epic*), then the gods would go hungry and thirsty.

In the Bible it is never implied that God is dependent on food and drink offerings for sustenance, but the presentation of food offerings before God was nevertheless a central feature of worship throughout the Old Testament. Only in the later books of the Old Testament, and in the New Testament, is it explained that God is not really interested in the offering itself, but in the heart of the worshipper. Therefore, we can see that the Sumerian belief that man was created solely to serve the gods would largely have been accepted by the writers of Genesis.

A third point of similarity between Genesis 2 and Eridu theology is seen in the Sumerian myth *Enki and the organization of the Earth*. This describes how Enki prepares the land of Mesopotamia for human habitation. For example, he ploughs the land for agriculture, builds houses, creates the wild beasts of the steppes, and establishes sheep herds in their pens. These preparations echo the Lord God's planting of the Garden of Eden for the benefit of mankind in Genesis 2.

Finally, there is another theme associated with the Garden of Eden that is shared by both Sumerian and biblical literature: the concept of Paradise itself.

Paradise is simply the ancient word for a garden, and the most important plant in the Garden of Eden is the Tree of Life, whose fruit bestows immortality. Since the *Epic of Gilgamesh* describes the quest of its hero for the lost secret of immortality, it is not surprising that this work contains some of the strongest echoes of the biblical theology of the Tree of Life. However, as noted above, the Epic was actually based almost entirely on a series of Sumerian short stories. Therefore, the Epic serves to help scholars understand these earlier Sumerian stories and fills gaps in the more fragmentary Sumerian versions.

The *Gilgamesh Epic* begins with the quest for immortality through deeds of valour. After describing the grandeur of the city of Uruk, the story explains the origin of Gilgamesh's 'sparring partner' Enkidu (tablet 1). This leads to an account of how Gilgamesh and Enkidu embark on a quest to kill a ferocious monster named Huwawa (or Humbaba) who possessed the power of human speech (Figure 10.3). This tale (tablets 2-5) is based on the Sumerian story '*Gilgamesh and Huwawa*', also known as '*Gilgamesh and the Land of the Living*'.

The story describes how Gilgamesh travels to a kind of enchanted forest of 'Erin' trees known as the Land of the Living. This forest contained a mountain that was the dwelling place of the gods, and was guarded (on the authority of Enlil) by a ferocious monster. The details of the battle are lacking, due to several missing sections, but somehow Gilgamesh succeeded in killing Humbaba, and then proceeded to cut down the trees of the forest. The Akkadian epic places the forest in Lebanon, but the Sumerian original places it to the East of Mesopotamia. The meaning of 'Erin' tree remains unclear, but the same word is used for the roof beams of buildings. It is normally taken to mean cedar or pine, but the word could relate more to the polished appearance of this wood than its type. This polished appearance would be consistent with the enchanted nature of the forest.

Figure 10.3. Babylonian clay mask of the monster Huwawa that was slain by Gilgamesh. The design, simulating animal intestines, gives the mask a grotesque appearance. Height 7 cm. British Museum.

This story seems to be a 'twisted' version of the tradition that gave rise to the story of the Fall of Man in Genesis Chapter 3. In that story, mankind was driven out of the enchanted garden that contained the Tree of Life, and cherubim and a flashing sword were placed in front of the garden to guard the way to the tree of life. The motif of a sacred tree that is tended by cherubim is common in Mesopotamian art, including several bas-relief carvings from Assyrian palaces (Figure 10.4). In addition, the location of the sacred forest in the East (in the Sumerian version) is consistent with the location of the land of immortality (Dilmun) in the east. Therefore, it appears that in the story *Gilgamesh and Humbaba*, the hero is trying to force his way into Paradise by killing the monster that guards it. Having done so, he cuts down the sacred trees and takes their wood back to Uruk. The wood was probably intended for the construction of a sacred door-way (tablet 7).

Figure 10.4. Sacred tree tended and guarded by winged beings resembling cherubim. Wall relief from the palace of Nimrud. British Museum.

The next Sumerian story in the Epic is *Gilgamesh and the Bull of Heaven* (tablet 6). When Gilgamesh returns from his victory over Humbaba, the goddess Ishtar (Inanna) asks Gilgamesh to be her lover. However, Gilgamesh knows that Ishtar is an adulteress who kills her lovers, so he refuses her advances. In revenge, Ishtar asks her father Anu to give her the Bull of Heaven to trample Gilgamesh to death. Looking at this punishment from another point of view, Enkidu sees the attack by the Bull of Heaven as the revenge of the gods for the slaying of Humbaba. Nevertheless, Gilgamesh and Enkidu also succeed in killing the Bull of Heaven (Figure 10.5). This creates a kind of symmetry, whereby Gilgamesh and Enkidu have together killed both of the 'pet' monsters belonging respectively to Enlil and Anu. They have thus 'thrown down the gauntlet' against the supreme gods of the pantheon.

In revenge for the killing of the Bull of Heaven, the gods decree that Enkidu must die (tablets 7-8). This section of the epic may have originated from the story *Gilgamesh, Enkidu and the Underworld* and it leads to the attempt by Gilgamesh to save Enkidu by discovering the secret of immortality. After mourning Enkidu's death (tablet 8), Gilgamesh begins his quest (tablet 9) by travelling to the land of immortality. This involves crossing the river of death (table 10) to reach the land of Dilmun where the immortalized Flood Hero (Ut-napishtim) lives. This finally leads to the climax of the Epic, in which Ut-napishtim explains how he achieved immortality by his obedience to Enki in building the Ark (tablet 11).

Figure 10.5. Gilgamesh and Enkidu kill the Bull of Heaven. Impression of a neo-Assyrian cylinder seal. For the sake of clarity, a group of vultures hovering over the bull was omitted from the drawing. British Museum.

After the telling of the Flood Story, the epic continues (tablet 11) by describing a trial that Gilgamesh must endure to show that he is worthy to gain immortality. To pass the test, he must resist sleep for a week. If he can resist the 'temporary death' of sleep, he will be able to conquer the 'permanent sleep' of death. However, Gilgamesh fails the test, and actually falls asleep for a whole week. Initially, Gilgamesh denies his failure, but Ut-napishtim 'proves' that Gilgamesh has slept for a whole week by showing him the loaves of 'daily bread' that were baked for him during his slumber . . . these loaves are so old that they have gone moldy!

Although he has failed the test of immortality, Gilgamesh is given one last chance of eternal life. Ut-napishtim knows of a prickly 'plant of rejuvenation' that may be recovered by diving to the bottom of the Apsu. This secret is his parting gift to Gilgamesh, who successfully recovers the plant and begins his journey home, taking the precious plant with him. However, on the way home, Gilgamesh sees an inviting pool of cool water and decides to take a bathe. He leaves the plant of rejuvenation on the shore, but its fragrance attracts a snake which eats the plant. By immediately casting its skin, the serpent shows that it has received the power of supernatural rejuvenation (Figure 10.6), and has also denied that power to Gilgamesh.

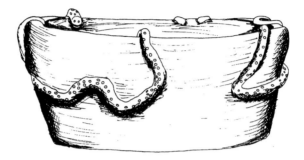

Figure 10.6. Ritual trough from the late Third Millennium of northern Mesopotamia in Syria, bearing serpents as symbols of supernatural power. British Museum.

The story of the 'plant of rejuvenation' is clearly related to the story of the supernatural trees of the Garden of Eden (Genesis Ch 3). Eve was deceived by the serpent and tempted to eat the forbidden fruit of the Knowledge of Good and Evil, after which she was prohibited from eating the fruit of the Tree of Life. In a similar way, Gilgamesh is cheated out of immortality by a serpent who takes advantage of a moment of human weakness. However, Gilgamesh has actually 'missed the point' of the biblical story of the Garden of Eden. In this story, the Tree of Life is only a metaphor for the rejuvenation which comes from communion with the True God. When Gilgamesh tries to 'force his way' into Paradise by killing the churubim that guard the Tree of Life, he is actually making enemies of the very gods (Anu and Enlil) who can give the gift of eternal life. There is no such thing as 'secular immortality' in isolation from God. Therefore, Gilgamesh will have to make do instead with the 'proxy immortality' of famous deeds and monuments of architecture (tablet 12).

Chapter 11

From Babel to Abraham

The stories about Gilgamesh originated in a period of intense struggle in Sumerian history, when the champion Gilgamesh was defending Uruk against the onslaught of the Semitic kings of Kish from the north. Gone now was the unquestioned supremacy which Uruk had demonstrated at the end of the Fourth Millennium. In its place, petty rivalries arose between several city states, each competing for brief periods of supremacy over the plain.

The idea of a lost 'golden age' when all was peace and harmony, replaced by a 'modern' state of conflict and division, was the theme of a Sumerian story first translated by Samuel Noah Kramer in 1944:

> In those days the land of Shubur (East),
> the place of plenty, of righteous decrees,
> Harmony-tongued Sumer (South),
> the great land of the "decrees of princeship"
> Uri (North), the land of all that is needful
> The land Martu (West), resting in security,
> The whole universe, the people in unison,
> To Enlil in one tongue gave praise.
>
> [Kramer, 1944]

Over twenty years later, Kramer published and translated the next piece of the story which had been found in the meantime:

> Then . . . Enki, the lord of abundance, (whose) commands are trustworthy,
> The lord of wisdom, who understands the land,
> The leader of the gods, endowed with wisdom, the lord of Eridu,
> Changed the speech of their mouths, brought contention into it,
> Into the speech of man that had been one.
>
> [Kramer, 1968]

On the basis of this translation, Kramer argued that the Sumerians believed that there had once been a period of universal harmony, which was brought to an end by

Enki, god of wisdom, possibly because of a rivalry between the gods. However, Genesis also speaks of a period of universal peace and understanding that was brought to an end when God scattered mankind and brought confusion into his language:

> Now the whole world had one language and a common speech. As men moved from the east, they found a plain in Shinar and settled there. . . . Then they said, "Come, let us build ourselves a city, with a tower that reaches to the heavens . . ." But the Lord came down to see the city and tower that the men were building. The Lord said, " . . . Come, let us go down and confuse their language so they will not understand each other." So the Lord scattered them from there over all the earth, and they stopped building the city.
>
> [Genesis 11:1-8]

According to this account, God's act of scattering mankind was in response to Man's ambition to build '*a tower that reaches to the heavens*'. This tower was said to be at Babylon, where the great ziggurat of Marduk was one of the principal monuments of Babylonian civilization through much of the Second Millennium BC (Figure 11.1).

Figure 11.1. A reconstruction of the great ziggurat of Babylon. Drawing of a model in the Staatliche Museen, Berlin.

In the Bible, Babylon came to symbolize the rebellion of mankind against the True God, and the Tower of Babel was therefore a potent symbol. Based on this symbol, the biblical story makes use of the similar sound of the name *Babhel* (Babylon) and the Hebrew word *balal* meaning 'confused', to create a very effective pun on the confusion of human speech. However, it is clear that the tradition concerning the end of the golden age of civilization dates from a much earlier time than the ziggurat of Babylon, which did not even exist until the beginning of the Second Millennium. Therefore, we must see the biblical story of the Tower of Babel as a deliberate anachronism, which brings together in one story two events that actually occurred more than a thousand years apart.

The real origin of both the Sumerian and biblical stories of a 'lost golden age' probably dates to the decline of Uruk, at the beginning of the Third Millennium BC, when the Semitic kings of Kish first challenged the supremacy of Uruk as the leading city of the ancient world. This period of division, when Sumerian speakers first clashed directly with their Semitic neighbours to the north, was preceded at Uruk by the rivalry between the two centres of temple worship, the so-called Anu Ziggurat dedicated to the God of Heaven, and the Eanna Complex dedicated to his consort and rival, Inanna, Queen of Heaven. It is clear that Inanna won the contest between the two cults, because the opening section of the *Gilgamesh Epic* refers to Eanna as the holiest sanctuary of Uruk, and to Ishtar (Inanna) as it patron. Consequently, the biblical reference to building '*a tower that reaches to the heavens*' was doubtless related to the building of Inanna's shrine of 'Eanna' (literally 'house of heaven') on top of a high tower.

This context for the story of Babel also explains the strange claim made by the Lord when he came down to see the tower (Gen 11:6):

"If as one people speaking the same language they have begun to do this,
    then nothing they plan to do will be impossible for them."

On the face of it, this claim seems to grossly overstate human invincibility. But in fact the economic power of the Eanna Complex at Uruk was so great that the cult of Inanna might have completely displaced the worship of the Cosmic Triad, so that the God of Heaven was no longer known in the earth. This threat was averted by an economic decline in the power of Uruk around 2750 BC. Hans Nissen suggested that this decline was actually caused by a change in the flow of the Euphrates river near present-day Baghdad, which caused a major diversion of water from its western channel to its eastern channel (Figure 6.6). As the last of the major cities to receive water from the western channel, Uruk would have been most affected by this change.

The decline of Uruk and the rise of a secular kingship at Kish spelled the end of the political power of the Temple elite. However, this did not imply a decline in the importance of religion in Mesopotamia, but an early form of 'Separation between Church and State'. For hand-in-hand with the appearance of kingship went the development of a new temple complex at Nippur ('place of Enlil') that would become the centre of religious worship for more than one city state, forming a kind of religious centre for the whole Mesopotamian plain. As the patron god of the Nippur temple, Enlil was now established as the effective head of the Sumerian pantheon, while Anu became a remote and shadowy figure.

The sacred precinct of Nippur contained temples devoted to several other deities, in addition to the E-kur or 'House of the Mountain' devoted to Enlil. Curiously enough, our most detailed knowledge about the history of these temples comes from an account referred to as the *Tummal Chronicle*, which records several episodes of building, decay, and repair of a temple dedicated to Ninlil, the 'wife' of Enlil.

The account has six cycles (Table 11.1) each of which describes, in a formulaic manner, the building of the temple by a certain king, its rise to pre-eminence under the king's son, and its subsequent fall into ruin, before it was renewed in the next cycle. These episodes stretch from around the time of Gilgamesh (the Early Dynastic period), through the great empire of Ur (the so-called Third Dynasty of Ur) until the waning period of Sumerian civilization at the beginning of the Old Babylonian period (the Isin Dynasty), a total of over 600 years (see Appendix 2).

Table 11.1. Table summarising the cycles of the *Tummal Chronicle*

Cycle	King	King's son	City of origin	Period
1	En-me-baragesi	Agga	Kish	ED II
2	Mesanne-padda	Meskiag-nunna	Ur	ED II
3	Gilgamesh	Ur-lugal	Uruk	ED II
4	Nanna	Meskiag-Nanna	Ur?	ED III?
5	Ur-Nammu	Shulgi	Ur	Ur III
6	Ishbi-Erra		Isin	Isin

One of the most traumatic periods in the history of Enlil's temple at Nippur was during the Empire of Akkad, when King Naram Sin demolished the temple in order to use its treasures to enrich the temple of Inanna at Akkad. According to the Sumerian lament, the *Curse of Akkad*, written during the Third Dynasty of Ur, Enlil punished the king for this desecration of his sanctuary by allowing waves of mountain savages (the Gutians) to invade the empire and reduce the city of Akkad to dust. In fact, the Gutians seem to have wiped Akkad completely off the map, because it is the only major city of ancient Mesopotamia that has never been rediscovered. In contrast, the temple of Enlil was rebuilt during the Third Dynasty of Ur, and subsequently continued as a major religious centre for hundreds of years, long after the Sumerians themselves had disappeared amongst waves of Semitic immigration.

The biblical patriarch Abraham was himself probably one of these Semitic immigrants, and according to Genesis, it is through him that we can trace the biblical story of origins back to its Mesopotamian roots. However, the account in Genesis was written after most of the temples of ancient Sumer had fallen into ruin. Therefore, the continuity of the Sumerian religious tradition, which we can trace in the archaeological record from Eridu to Uruk and thence to Nippur, is represented in Genesis using the schematic form of a patriarchal genealogy. In this way, the author of Genesis follows a tradition similar to the *Sumerian King List*, which traced the history of Sumerian civilization from Eridu to Isin in a stylized way as a series of kingly dynasties.

The thread of continuity between the biblical patriarchs is represented in Genesis by two major genealogies, each with ten generations (Table 11.2) which link Adam with Noah (Ch 5) and Shem with Abraham (Ch 11). The great life-spans of the biblical patriarchs, especially those before the Flood, resemble to a lesser degree the antediluvian rulers of the *Sumerian King List*. To many people, these incredible lifetimes cast doubt on the veracity of the Genesis text. However, Genesis gives clear pointers that these genealogies are not *meant* to be taken literally, but are a symbolic representation of the continuity of the religious experience of the patriarchs through centuries of Mesopotamian history and pre-history.

Table 11.2. Table comparing the genealogies of Adam and Shem.

Ch 5:3-32	Ch 11:1-26 (MT)	Ch11:1-26 (LXX)
Adam	(Noah)	Shem
Seth	Shem	Arphaxad
Enosh	Arphaxad	(Cainan)
Kenan	Shelah	Shelah
Mahalalel	Eber	Eber
Jared	Peleg	Peleg
Enoch	Reu	Reu
Methuselah	Serug	Serug
Lamech	Nahor	Nahor
Noah	Terah	Terah
Shem, Ham, Japheth	Abram, Nahor, Haran	Abram, Nahor, Haran

MT = Hebrew 'Masoretic' text. LXX = Greek 'Septuagint' translation.

A first line of evidence for the schematic form of these genealogies is the way in which Genesis Chapter 11 mirrors Chapter 5, both genealogies having a linear chain of ten generations which ends in a three-fold branch (Table 11.2). This symmetry is only fully achieved in the Hebrew ('Masoretic') text if Noah is included at the head of the Shemite genealogy (column 2). However, in the Greek ('Septuagint') translation of Genesis, the symmetry is more fully achieved by the insertion of an extra generation, whereby Cainan becomes Shem's grand-son (column 3).

Even stronger evidence for the schematic structure of these genealogies comes from the fact that the 'raw' material used to make them is still preserved elsewhere in Genesis. This is shown most clearly by the genealogy of Adam (Table 11.3).

The full genealogy of Adam (column 3) is found in Genesis Chapter 5, but the 'raw material' used to make it is still present in two shorter genealogies in Chapter 4. One of these genealogies describes the sons of Cain, and one describes the sons of Seth (Table 11.3, columns 1 and 2). Close comparison between the genealogy of Cain (column 1) and the more complete genealogy in Chapter 5 (column 3) shows that they are composed essentially of the same names, partially rearranged and with small variations in spelling. On the other hand, a major difference between these genealogies is their style of presentation. The genealogy of Chapter 5 has a rigid formalism, and, most notably, there is specific mention in Genesis 5:1 that it was a written record. In contrast, Cain's genealogy is presented in an anecdotal style that is typical of accounts handed down orally in story form. Hence, the formal genealogy in Chapter 5 was probably created by combining the two shorter genealogies of Chapter 4, even though these actually represent distinct lineages.

When we look in detail at the genealogy of Abraham, we can see indications of a similar process at work. For example, when we examine the last four generations of Abraham's genealogy (Table 11.4, column 2), we find that they are place names in northern Mesopotamia, where Abraham lived with his father after their family left the city of Ur in southern Mesopotamia. This implies that Abraham's family might have originated in Northen Mesopotamia, before moving to the city of Ur (Ur of the Chaldees). This short family genealogy was probably combined with a completely separate source, called the Table of Nations, which is preserved in Genesis Ch 10 (Table 11.4, column 1). Together, the two sources yielded a genealogy the same length as the one linking Adam with Noah.

Table 11.3. The three genealogies of Adam and how they are related.

Ch 4:17-22	Ch 4:25-26	Ch 5:3-32
Adam	Adam	Adam
|	Seth	Seth
|	Enosh	Enosh
Cain		Kenan
Enoch	---------------\ /-------------->	Mahalalel
Irad	X	Jared
Mehujael	---------------/ \-------------->	Enoch
Methusael		Methuselah
Lamech		Lamech
|		Noah
Jabal, Jubal, Tubal		Shem, Ham, Japheth

Table 11.4. Component parts of the genealogy of Abraham.

Genesis Ch 10:21-29	Settlement names	Genesis Ch 11:10-26
Shem		Shem
Arphaxad		Arphaxad
		(Cainan)
Shelah		Shelah
Eber		Eber
Peleg		Peleg
		Reu
	Serug	Serug
	Nahor	Nahor
	Terah	Terah
	Haran	Abram, Nahor, Haran

In trying to understand how the religious traditions of the Sumerians might have been passed down to Abraham, the genealogies in the Table of Nations are crucial. Overall, this Table gives a schematic account of the origins of Middle East people groups as descendants of Noah after the Flood. For example, the peoples of the northern Middle East and southeast Europe are attributed to the descendants of Japheth, the North Africans and Canaanites are attributed to the descendants of Ham, while the Assyrians, Arameans, Elamites and Hebrews are attributed to the descendants of Shem. However, notably absent from this list of peoples are the Sumerians.

Since other lines of evidence point to the Sumerians as the first pioneers of biblical religion, this omission is very ironic. However, even the Sumerians themselves seem to have lost sight of their own origins and identity. We can see this loss of identity when we examine late Third Millennium artistic representations of the Sumerians and their gods, which are commonly portrayed in 'introduction scenes'.

One of the most important examples of an introduction scene is a carved limestone bas-relief known as the Stele of Gudea (Figure 11.2). This stele shows the presentation of Gudea to one of the Great Gods by his patron deity. The figure of the great god is largely lost, but we can see the back of his throne, and based on the stream of water coming down in front of him, he was probably Enki. Gudea (on the far left) has the typical clean-shaven appearance of a Sumerian, and is wearing a typical Sumerian bordered gown, as was seen earlier on the Proto-literate age Uruk Vase (Figure 6.4). In contrast, all of the divine figures (indicated by their many-horned head-dresses) have long hair and beards, and are wearing a long pleated garment that was originally of Semitic origin. This form of Semitic dress probably became popular in Mesopotamia after the northern city of Kish achieved political dominance over the plain in the Early Dynastic period.

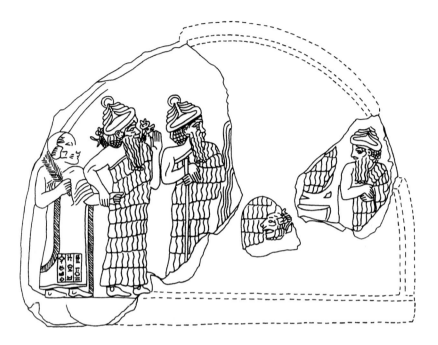

Figure 11.2. Stele of Gudea. Limestone bas-relief. Vorderasiatisches Museen, Berlin.

We know that the kings of Kish were Semitic, because several of their names are recognizable as words in the Akkadian language. However, when these kings achieved political dominance over Mesopotamia, they nevertheless adopted Sumerian religion as their own. A new temple was built at the city of Nippur, dedicated to Enlil, and this temple became the religious centre of Mesopotamia for more than 1000 years, not losing its dominance until the rise of Babylon under Hammurabi. Hence, even though the Cosmic Triad of Anu, Enlil and Enki was Sumerian in origin, the political dominance of the Semitic dynasty at Kish was so strong that the gods themselves 'adopted' the Semitic form of dress. Therefore, the gods of the Sumerians became so completely identified with the Semitic immigrants of northern Mesopotamia that in later times it appeared that the gods themselves were 'Semitic'.

So it was that by the time the Table of Nations was compiled, its author did not even know of the existence of the Sumerians. However, their existence is still betrayed in the Genesis text. For example, in the excerpt from Genesis 11:1 quoted above, we read:

Now the whole world had one language and a common speech.
As men moved from the east, they found a plain in Shinar and settled there.

This plain in *Shinar* is none other than Sumer itself, and it has been suggested by some scholars that even the name Shem was derived from Shumer (=Sumer). It would be a great irony if the very name 'Semitic' was etymologically derived from 'Sumerian', since these two people groups had languages as different as chalk and cheese. And yet it would also be appropriate, because the Sumerians were the *spiritual* forefathers of the Semitic peoples of the Middle East.

This spiritual heritage is represented in the genealogy of Shem (Table 11.5) by the line of descent through Arphaxad, Shelah and Eber, eventually leading to Abraham. The first of these names (Arphaxad) is probably Sumerian, whereas his son Shelah is immediately recognizable as Semitic, and his grandson Eber is the 'father' (eponymous ancestor) of the Hebrews. Hence, Genesis schematically describes the passing of Sumerian culture and religion to the Semitic peoples, and ultimately to the Hebrews.

Table 11.5. Genealogy of Shem from the Table of Nations (Gen Ch 10).

Shem				
Elam	Ashur	**Arphaxad**	Lud	Aram
(Elamites)	(Assyrians)		(?)	(Arameans)
		Shelah		
				4 sons named
		Eber (Hebrews)		
	Peleg		Joktan	
	(line to Abraham)			
	(in Gen Ch 11)		11 sons named	

In later times, the God of the Hebrews was called Yahweh (Jehovah), based on the revelation to Moses at the burning bush, described in the book of Exodus. However, the evidence from Genesis suggests that the God of the patriarchs, Abraham, Isaac and Jacob, was actually called El. For example, Abraham worshipped a god sometimes called El-elyon (The Lord Most High, Gen 14:19) and at other times called El-shaddai (The Lord who provides, Gen 17:1). Similarly, after a night-long struggle with the Angel of God (Gen 32:28), Jacob was named Israel, meaning 'He struggles with El'.

Most scholars have assumed that the patriarchs learned of this god El from the Canaanites, since the head of the Canaanite pantheon was also named El. However, in the Semitic tongue, El simply means Lord, so there is no direct association between the God of Abraham and the chief god of Canaanites. It is much more likely that *both* the patriarchal god El and the Canaanite god El were derived from the Mesopotamian god El-lil (=Enlil), who was the head of the Sumerian pantheon throughout the Third Millennium BC.

The Mesopotamian origins of the Canaanite god El are suggested in a cylinder seal from the Canaanite kingdom of Ugarit, an independent nation in the Middle East around the middle of the Second Millennium (ca. 1400 BC). This seal shows the local Canaanite thunder god, Baal, armed with a club and a (zig-zag) lightening-bolt. Facing Baal is another deity, thought to be the god El, who is wearing the pleated garment that was the characteristic mark of the gods of Mesopotamia (Figure 11.3). Interestingly, he also holds a vase from which two streams of water flow, and in which fish are swimming. This suggests that the Canaanite god El had subsumed into his character some of the attributes of the Sumerian god Enki (god of living waters), as well as Enlil (head of the Sumerian pantheon).

Figure 11.3. Ugaritic cylinder seal showing the Canaanites gods Baal and El, the latter dressed in the style of the chief gods of Mesopotamia.

Biblical evidence indicates that the Israelites also traced the origin of their god El to Mesopotamia. For example, when Stephen the Martyr addressed the Jewish Sanhedrin during the early development of the Christian Church (Acts 7:1), he began his history of the Jewish religion with the following words (italics mine):

> "Brothers and fathers, listen to me! The God of Glory appeared to our father Abraham *while he was still in Mesopotamia*, before he lived in Haran. 'Leave your country and your people,' God said, 'and go to the land I will show you.'"

Hence, we can conclude that the revelation of the Hebrew god El, later known as Yahweh, began in Mesopotamia, where it must have occurred in the context of the religious worship that Abraham had already experienced. And this religious experience was itself the legacy of the Sumerians.

Chapter 12

The Spiritual Big Bang

Having traced how the religion of the Sumerians may have been passed down to us, we are left with the question of how this religious experience began. Biblical and Mesopotamian sources provide different kinds of insights about this, but if we can successfully combine them, they may shed more light on the question than either source alone.

The most explicit account of the origin of Mesopotamian civilization is presented at the beginning of a book on Babylonian history called the *Babyloniaca*. This work was written in Greek around 281 BC by a priest of Marduk called Berossos, and was an attempt to present the Mesopotamian world view to the Greeks, after the conquest of the Middle East by Alexander the Great. Unfortunately, the Greeks displayed little interest in the *Babyloniaca* because they found the view of history that it presented to be inherently unbelievable. This history attributed Babylonian civilization to a host of 'divine decrees' handed down from the gods at the time the world began, and then linked this primaeval history to the more modern world using a version of the *Sumerian King List*. However, the Greeks believed that civilization had been created by human endeavour over a period of thousands of years, and they considered the quotations from the King List to be incredible (especially the extreme reigns of the kings who ruled before the Flood).

Because of the lack of interest in the *Babyloniaca* in the ancient Greek world, all of the original copies of the work were lost. However, an abridgement of it was made by a Greco-Roman scholar, Cornelius Polyhistor, in the first century AD. This work was also lost, except for excerpts made in the early 4th century AD by the Christian scholar Eusabius. Even this work was lost, but Polyhistor's quotes of the *Babyloniaca* were preserved in the *Chronographia* of George Syncellus. The main reason that the *Babyloniaca* was quoted by these historians was to show how obviously *unbelievable* it was. However, now that much of the original cuneiform literature has been recovered, we can see that the *Babyloniaca* was a fairly accurate account of what the Babylonians considered to be their ancient history. For example, the list of kings who reigned before the Flood quoted in the *Babyloniaca* has strong resemblances to much older versions of the *Sumerian King List*, such as the Weld Blundell prism (Figure 7.1).

Although the ancient Mesopotamian myths contain only confused snap-shots of the origins of their civilization, we now have a much better understanding of how to interpret these ancient sources in order to obtain historical information from them. Therefore, we will now examine the reconstructed opening section of the *Babyloniaca,* in order to understand its view of the origins of Sumerian religion. After briefly describing the climate and produce of Mesopotamia, it is thought that Berossos began his history as follows:

> There was a great crowd of men in Babylonia and they lived without laws just as wild animals. In the first year, a beast named Oannes appeared from the Erythraean Sea (Persian Gulf) in a place adjacent to Babylonia. Its entire body was that of a fish, but a human head had grown beneath the head of the fish and human feet likewise had grown from the fish's tail. It also had a human voice. A picture of it is still preserved today. This beast spent the days with the men but ate no food. It gave to the men the knowledge of letters and sciences and crafts of all types. It also taught them how to found cities, establish temples, introduce laws and measure land. It also revealed to them seeds and the gathering of fruits, and in general it gave men everything which is connected with the civilized life. From the time of that beast, nothing further has been discovered. But when the sun set, this beast Oannes plunged back into the sea and spent the night in the deep, for it was amphibious.
>
> [Translation: Burstein, 1978]

Despite the far-fetched nature of this account, the tradition of the 'fish men' is quite widely known in Assyrian and Babylonian sources of the First Millennium BC. For example, a *picture still preserved today* is seen in a wall relief from the royal palace at Khorsabad (Figure 12.1). In addition, there are numerous other depictions of the

Figure 12.1. Swimming fish-man. Detail of a stone relief from the palace of Sargon II at Khorsabad. Musée du Louvre.

'fish men' in Assyrian art, including bas-relief carvings from the temple of the god Ninurta at Nimrud, along with various cylinder seals and clay figurines.

We cannot be certain how much of the legend of the Fish Men goes back to the Sumerians, but they are mentioned in the Akkadian epic poem *Erra and Ishum*, which dates from around the same period (the eighth century BC) as the Assyrian wall reliefs. The relevant lines are as follows:

> Where are the seven sages of the Apsu, the holy carp,
> who are perfect in lofty wisdom like Ea (Enki) their lord.?
> [Translation: Dalley, 1989]

This excerpt suggests that a mysterious group of semi-divine beings, referred to as the Seven Sages, were synonymous with the Fish Men. However, elsewhere, it appears that the Seven Sages were seven wise kings who were the *recipients* of supernatural wisdom.

The story of the first of the Seven Sages is spelled out in more detail in the Akkadian myth of *Adapa*. This myth is known in fragmentary form, based on late Second Millennium tablets from Ashur in Assyria and from El-Amarna in Egypt (along with diplomatic communications written in Akkadian cuneiform). The myth begins by relating how Adapa, a 'son of Eridu' was made a sage by Enki, god of wisdom:

> He (Enki) made broad understanding perfect in him (Adapa),
> To disclose the design of the Land.
> To him he gave wisdom, but did not give eternal life
> At that time, in those years, he was a sage, son of Eridu.
> [Translation: Dalley, 1989]

The myth goes on to explain that Adapa became the chief priest of the Eridu temple, in charge of all the offerings of bread, water and fish in the temple. (Remains of fish have indeed been found on the altar in the oldest temple ruins in Eridu). The remaining part of the myth describes how Adapa went out fishing to obtain offerings for the temple of Enki, and how his boat sank when the South Wind created a storm. As Adapa was drowning, he cursed the South Wind, breaking its wing. Adapa was then summoned to heaven (perhaps after his death) and appeared before Anu, where he was commanded to give an account of his actions. However, two gods interceded on Adapa's behalf (as patron deities), so that Anu was placated. Anu then exclaimed:

> Why did Enki disclose to wretched mankind
> The ways of Heaven and Earth, give them a heavy heart?
> It was he (Enki) who did it! What can we do for him (Adapa)?
> Fetch him the Bread of Life and let him eat.

However, Adapa declined the offer of the Bread of Life because he had been told by Enki that he would be offered poison by Anu. As a result, Adapa lost the chance of eternal life, and was sent back to the Earth.

Since this story predates the myth of *Erra and Ishum*, it is probably closer to the Sumerian view of the origins of their civilization, and implies that the sages were the human recipients of divine wisdom, rather than supernatural beings or divine messengers. In any case, it is clear that the source of their revelation was Enki, God of Wisdom and Friend of Man, who is always identified as the giver of the divine decrees of civilization (referred to in the myth as 'the ways of heaven and earth') . Based on his role as the first priest of Eridu, the recipient of divine wisdom, and the one who lost the gift of eternal life, Adapa has often been regarded as the Mesopotamian equivalent of the biblical Adam.

One of the first things that we might expect the God of Wisdom to have revealed to mankind is the story of Creation, as presented in Genesis Chapter 1. However, this story presents an obstacle to the modern reader because it speaks of the creation of the Heavens and the Earth in six days. Although this may have been taken as a literal account by ancient peoples, scientific evidence amassed over the past 200 years shows overwhelmingly that the Earth was not created in six literal days. Hence, many attempts have been made to harmonize the Genesis account of creation with scientific evidence for an ancient Earth.

One of the most popular 'solutions' to this problem is the 'day-age' theory, whereby each 'day' of Genesis 1 is argued to represent a long Geological age in the history of the Earth. However, many features of the Genesis account are incompatible with the 'day-age' theory, such as the creation of light on day one and plants on day three, before the sun and moon on day four. These 'mis-fits' are not surprising, because Genesis 1 is a *pre-scientific* account, which we should not expect to fit into a modern scientific framework. Instead, we should see Genesis 1 as a *theological* statement about the creation, which is structured to explain its relationship to God. We can then see that the six days of creation form two triads, as shown in Table 12.1. Each of these triads addresses one aspect of the primordial state of the Earth. Its formlessness is changed into order by creative acts of separation between the realms of the cosmos (column 1). Its emptiness is then changed into abundance by creative acts of population in each realm (column 2).

Table 12.1. The double triad structure of Genesis Chapter 1

Acts of separation	Acts of population
Light and darkness (v 3-5)	Heavenly lights (v 14-19)
Water above and below the sky (v 6-8)	Fish in water and birds in sky (v 20-23)
Land environment and the sea (v 9-13)	Land animals and mankind (v 24-31)

Evidence that the days of creation are 24-hour human days, and not geological ages, is provided by the phrase *'There was evening and there was morning'* at the end of each day. However, if we reject the day-age theory, this begs the question of what happened on the 'six days of creation', if it was not the creation of the Earth?

One of the most insightful explanations of this mystery was proposed by P. J. Wiseman, in his book *Clues to Creation in Genesis*. Wiseman suggested that the 'six days' of Genesis 1 were not days of *creation* but days of *revelation*. Thus, in six human days, God revealed to Adam the origins of the Heavens and the Earth, after which the seventh day was proclaimed by God as a day of rest. But what form might this revelation have taken?

In the stories of the Patriarchs, Abraham, Isaac and Jacob, there are several accounts of the appearance of God in human form (e.g. Gen 17:1-3; 18:1-2; 32:30), sometimes referred to as the 'Angel of the Lord'. In such cases it is often not quite clear whether the figure is indeed an angel (messenger of God), or the Lord himself, in human form. In other instances, God appeared in a supernatural form, such as in the 'burning bush' seen by Moses (Exodus 3:2).

The Mesopotamian legend of the Fish Man is probably a corrupted version of this type of tradition, to the extent that the divine revelation was perhaps carried by a figure who was apparently human, but came from the sea in a supernatural manner. This duality is well captured by a bas-relief from the temple of Ninurta at Nimrud (Figure 12.2), which shows a Fish Man in a guise similar to that normally used for cherubim, another type of supernatural being known from both Mesopotamian and biblical sources.

The claim by Berossos that the Fish Man appeared out of the Erythraean Sea is consistent with the Sumerian tradition that there was a Land of Immortality, located on a supernatural island mountain called Dilmun, across the Eastern Sea (the Persian Gulf). As noted earlier, Dilmun was believed to be the resting place of the Flood Hero, who received eternal life as a reward for his obedience in building the Ark. In later Sumerian times (the time of the Third Dynasty of Ur), Dilmun became identified with the island of Bahrein in the Persian Gulf. At this time, the belief in Bahrein as the 'Isle of the Blessed' was so strong that hundreds of thousands of Sumerians had their remains transported there for burial, in the hopes of rising from the dead in the very land of immortality. This has left the island pockmarked by vast fields of tumulus-type burial mounds.

Even though there is a surprising degree of agreement between biblical and Mesopotamian sources about the manifestation of supernatural beings to mankind, many people might still question the evidence that an actual man called Adam really existed. However, every religious movement has had a human originator who received a divine revelation, and in this case, the name of the originator, Adam, is simply the Semitic word for 'the man'. So we can see that some kind of '*adam*' must have existed, and therefore, why not the biblical Adam? After all, the Bible says that revelation began in lower Mesopotamia, where the Tigris and Euphrates meet, and we have seen that archaeological evidence clearly points to this area as the fount of human civilization, where the first cities were gathered round temples of divine worship . . .

Figure 12.2. Bas relief carving of a Fish Man from the temple of Ninurta at Nimrud, erected by the Assyrian king Ashur-nasirpal II. Based on an engraving by Layard (1849).

Chapter 13

Paradise lost and regained

One person who gave a lot of thought to the existence of Adam was C. S. Lewis, Oxford don and author of the *Narnia* children's fantasy novels. Lewis often used to meet with friends and colleagues to have literary discussions, and his biographer, A. N. Wilson, records one such evening when the conversation at dinner turned to an interesting question: Which literary or historical figure would each of them most look forward to meeting after death? Various names were mentioned, including Shakespeare and St Paul. However, when it came to Lewis' turn, he unhesitatingly declared his preference to meet Adam, for reasons he had outlined several years previously in his book on Milton, *A Preface to 'Paradise Lost'*:

> Adam was, from the first, a man in knowledge as well as in stature. He alone of all men 'had been in Eden, in the garden of God, he had walked up and down in the midst of the stones of fire'. He was endowed, says Athanasius, with 'a vision of God so far-reaching that he could contemplate the eternity of the Divine Essence and the cosmic operations of His Word'.

However, in response to Lewis' suggestion, a colleague from the English Department named Helen Gardner replied that she was not the least bit interested in meeting Adam, since if he actually existed, the 'first man' must have been a 'Neanderthal ape-like figure, whose conversation she could not conceive of finding interesting.' This response apparently brought a stony silence on the assembled group, until Lewis himself gruffly replied, 'I see we have a Darwinian in our midst.'

This dispute between theological and scientific world views is typical of the wider debate between Faith and Science. But the mistake of regarding Adam as some kind of Neanderthal is caused by a failure to distinguish between the first man who had a relationship with God, and the first member of the human genus or human species. The Darwinian account of man, as far as it goes, is only half the story of the human race, since it cannot comprehend the spiritual component of Man. Genesis does not claim that Adam was the first member of the human species; but it does say that he was the first fully complete man.

But if Adam had tasted immortality, and had spoken with God 'face to face' (Saint Ambrose), then he should have known the character of God in at least as

many facets as we do in today's imperfect world. And since the three persons of the
Godhead are an intrinsic aspect of the character of God, surely Adam also knew
God as a Trinity of three divine persons? This was the belief of the early Church
Father, Athanasius of Alexandria, quoted above by C. S. Lewis.

Athanasius lived from 295 to 373 AD, and was instrumental in the framing of
the Nicean Creed, which established the doctrine of the Holy Trinity in AD 325.
Athanasius argued that the doctrine of the Trinity was not only based on the New
Testament witness to the divinity of Jesus Christ (the Word made flesh), but was
also established by three crucial texts in Genesis (Ch 1:26, 3:22 and 11:7) where
God speaks in the plural; "Let us make man in our image"; "The man has now
become like one of us"; and "Let us go down and confuse their language". There
is every reason why a later Monotheist editor of Genesis might have wanted to
render these quotes in the singular, but presumably (and correctly) he was afraid to
change the very Word of God spoken.

As well as this evidence for the Trinity, Genesis also provides evidence for a
continuity of divine worship from Adam, through the Flood Hero, to Abraham, the
Father of the Jewish and Christian faiths. But it is hardly credible that this continuity
of divine worship could have existed in some kind of 'hermit colony' outside the
rest of human civilization. On the contrary, the combination of the biblical and
Mesopotamian evidence strongly suggests that human worship of the True God was
preserved as a golden thread that ran through the very centre of ancient Mesopotamian culture, from the era before the Flood to the Sumerians, from them to the
Semitic peoples, and finally to Abraham.

So it should not be surprising that the three divine persons of the Trinity
correspond in their roles to the 'Sumerian Holy Trinity' represented by the Cosmic
Triad. Firstly, the position of Anu as the heavenly father of the Mesopotamian
pantheon mirrors the role of the biblical Heavenly Father. Secondly, the image of
Enlil as the Lord, Breath of God, is consistent with the role of the Holy Spirit who
carries out the will of the Father on the Earth. Thirdly, the role of Enki as the god
of wisdom, the god of living waters, and the saviour of mankind, reflects the role
of the Son of God.

The concept of 'three Gods in one' should have been as accessible to the
ancient world as it is to us, but instead, the Sumerian Holy Trinity was 'duplicated'
by a corrupt priesthood to produce a Pagan Trinity of astral deities, represented by
the sun, moon and stars. Thus began the plethora of divinities that soon grew into
the Sumerian pantheon, and which was passed from the Sumerians to the Amorites,
Canaanites, Phoenicians, Greeks and Romans. At the same time, the unity of the
Trinity was lost as the Cosmic Triad splintered into three separate gods, and the
identity of each member gradually became confused and corrupted. Anu became
such a remote figure that he was almost inaccessible, whereas Enlil and Enki were
'reduced' to a human scale and labelled as lecherous womanizers.

In response to the corruption of the Holy Trinity, the revelation to Moses at the
burning bush emphasized the unity of the Godhead as a single deity. This revelation was proclaimed in the First Commandment (Deuteronomy 6:4; Mark 12:29):

"Hear O Israel: The LORD our God, the LORD is one."

But, just as the unity of the Trinity was broken by the Sumerian priesthood into polytheism, so the singularity of God was over-emphasized by the Pharisees of Jesus' day, leading them to crucify the Son of God.

This tension between God as Trinity and God as Unity is parallelled in the New Testament by the tension between God as Judge and God as Saviour of mankind. Significantly, the same tension is also found in the Mesopotamian Flood Story, where Anu and Enlil bring the catastrophe of the Flood, but Enki, the Friend of Mankind, mitigates its effect by showing the Flood Hero that he can be saved by obedience to the divine command. Unable to reconcile these actions of the Cosmic Triad within a single Godhead, the Mesopotamian tradition separated them into three competing deities. However, the *original* character of Enki was not a 'Pagan Christ' but part of the revelation of the Holy Trinity to Adam.

But even though it was the God of wisdom who revealed to mankind the divine decrees of civilization (symbolized by the Tree of Knowledge of Good and Evil), he also warned Adam not to eat its fruit (the power of independent choice and action). Unfortunately, after his enlightenment, Adam could not resist the temptation of eating the fruit of independence, and in that day he was cut off from intimacy with the True God. This has led to mankind's endless attempt to reach out for God, and thus regain the secret of eternal life.

Because the dwelling of God was believed to be in the Holy Place at the top of the Temple Mountain, many visionaries throughout history have seen the restoration of spiritual relationship with God as the ascent up a cosmic mountain or ziggurat to a paradisaical garden where God lives in communion with man. Perhaps the earliest record of such a vision is the dream of Jacob the Patriarch as he slept with his head on a stone pillow at Bethel (Gen 28:12):

> He had a dream in which he saw a stairway resting on the earth, with its top reaching to heaven, and the angels of God were ascending and descending on it. There above it stood the LORD, and he said: "I am the LORD, the God of your father Abraham and the God of Isaac . . ."

This vision perfectly describes the Great Stairway of a Mesopotamian ziggurat, such as Jacob's mother Rebekah must have described to him from her childhood memories of Haran in northern Mesopotamia. The temple priests would ascend and descend on this stairway (Figure 13.1), just as the angels were seen to do in Jacob's dream; and at the summit of the stairs would be the house that was the very dwelling place of the Divine Presence. After the dream, Jacob exclaimed "How awesome is this place! This is none other than the house of God; this is the gate of heaven." In saying this he was thinking in quite concrete terms of the reality of being in the manifest presence of God.

The medieval poet, Dante Alighieri, had a similar vision of the restoration of spiritual communication between Man and God as the climbing of a 'Mountain of

Figure 13.1. View up the great stairway of the partially-reconstructed ziggurat of Ur.

Purgatory'. He describes it in the middle book (*Purgatorio*) of his epic work '*The Divine Comedy*', completed in 1321. After ascending many levels of the mountain of Purgatory, which again seems to be reminiscent of a Mesopotamian ziggurat, Dante found himself at the summit of the mountain, entering an enchanted forest which was a recreation of the Garden of Eden. The cosmic mountain is envisaged in an illustration from a 15th century edition of the Divine Comedy in Figure 13.2.

A vision similar to Dante's was described recently by Rick Joyner under the title '*The Final Quest*'. In his vision, Rick Joyner saw a 'Holy Mountain', also with many terraces. As a soldier in God's army, Joyner saw himself ascending this mountain at the same time as he fought in a great battle against the powers of darkness, including demons, vultures and serpents. The following quote comes from the middle of this battle, and describes how he reached the top of the cosmic mountain:

> Since there seemed to be little that we could do now against the enemy we decided to just try to climb as far as we could until we found something that would work against the serpents.
>
> We passed levels of truth very fast. On most of them we did not even bother to look around if there was not a weapon apparent that would work on the serpents. . . .

Figure 13.2. Dante presents his vision of the mountain of Purgatory, with the Garden of Eden at its summit. Simplified from an illustrated 15th century edition of *The Divine Comedy*.

Almost without warning we came to a level that opened up into a garden. It was the most beautiful place I had ever seen. Over the entrance to this garden was written "The Father's Unconditional Love." This entrance was so glorious and inviting that we could not resist entering. As soon as I entered I saw a tree that I knew was the Tree of Life. It was in the middle of this garden, and it was still guarded by angels of awesome power and authority. . . . They seemed friendly, as if they had been expecting us. . . . One of the angels called out, "Those who make it to this level, who know the Father's love, can eat."

I did not know how hungry I was. When I tasted the fruit, it was better than anything I had ever tasted, but it was, also, somehow familiar. It brought memories of sunshine, rain, beautiful fields, the sun setting over the ocean, but even more than that, of the people I loved. With every bite I loved everything and everyone more. Then my enemies started coming to mind, and I loved them, too. The feeling was soon greater than anything I had ever experienced . . . Then I heard the voice of the Lord, saying, "This is now your daily bread. It shall never be withheld from you. You may eat as much and as often as you like. There is no end to my love."

~

Appendices

Appendix 1. Sumerian and Akkadian names of major Mesopotamian gods

Sumerian	Akkadian	Attributes
Great gods, based on kudurru		
Nanna	Sin	Moon god
Utu	Shamash	Sun god
Inanna	Ishtar	Venus, Queen of Heaven, goddess of love and war
An	Anu	God of Heaven, Father of the gods
En-lil	El-lil	Lord of the air/wind/breath
En-ki	Ea	Lord of the Earth, god of wisdom & sweet water
–	Marduk	God of Babylon
–	Nabu	God of writing
Ninhursaga	Mami	Mother goddess
Other gods and goddesses		
Ninurta	Adad/Dagan	Thunder-god
Ninlil		Wife of En-lil

Appendix 2. Summary of Major Periods of Mesopotamian History

C-14 age B.C.	Name of Period in Mesopotamia		General name of Period
540			
	Neo Babylonian Empire		
630			
	Neo Assyrian Empire		Iron age
930			
	Second Assyrian Empire		
1200	First Babylonian Empire		
	First Assyrian Empire		
			Late Bronze
	Kassites		
1600			
	Old	Babylon	
	Babylonian	Larsa	Middle Bronze
	Period	Isin	
2020			
	3rd Dynasty of Ur		
2200	Gutian period		
	Akkadian Dynasty		
2370			
		III	
2600	Early		
	Dynastic	II	Early Bronze
2750	Period		
		I	
3000			
	Proto-literate (Jemdet Nasr)		
3200			
		Late	
3600	Uruk		Chalcolithic
		Early	
4000			
		Late	
4500	Ubaid		
		Early	
5400			Neolithic
		Late	
5700	Halaf		
		Early	
6100			

(In some nomenclature, the Ubaid period overlaps with the Halaf)

Bibliography

This bibliography lists sources specifically cited in the text, along with others that provide important background to ideas discussed in this book. More detailed citations are given in the author's book '*On a Faraway Day . . . A New View of Genesis in Ancient Mesopotamia*'. For references with two quoted dates, the first represents the earliest edition (sometimes in a foreign language), while the later date represents the edition consulted by the present author, and is the one for which page numbers are given.

Adkins, A. (2003/2004). *Empires of the Plain: Henry Rawlinson and the Lost Languages of Babylon*. HarperCollins. 424 p.

Aksu, A. E., Hiscott, R. N. and Yasar, D. (1999). Oscillating Quaternary water levels of the Marmara Sea and vigorous outflow into the Aegean Sea from the Marmara Sea–Black Sea drainage corridor. *Marine Geology* 153, 275-302.

Alster, B. (1976). On the earliest Sumerian literary tradition. *J. Cuneiform Studies* 28, 109-126.

Athanasius, In: Thomson, R. W. (Ed., 1971). *Contra Gentes* and *De Incarnatione*. Oxford Univ. Press, 288 p.

Ballard, R. D., Hiebert, F. T., Coleman, D. F. and 7 others (2001). Deepwater archaeology of the Black Sea: the 2000 season at Sinop, Turkey. *American J. Archaeology* 105, 607-623.

Bar-Matthews, M., Ayalon, A. and Kaufman, A. (1997). Late quaternary paleoclimate in the Eastern Mediterranean region from stable isotope analysis of speleothems at Soreq Cave, Israel. *Quaternary Research* 47, 155-168.

Bar-Matthews, M., Ayalon, A. and Kaufman, A. (2000). Timing and hydrological conditions of Sapropel events in the Eastern Mediterranean, as evident from speleothems, Soreq Cave, Israel. *Chem. Geol.* 169, 145-156.

Barnett, R. D. (1966/68). *Illustration of Old Testament History*. British Museum. 91 p.

Biggs, R. D. (1966). The Abu Salabikh tablets. *J. Cuneiform Studies* 20, 73-88.

Biggs, R. D. (1974). *Inscriptions from Tell Abu Salabikh*. Chicago: Oriental Institute Publications 99, 122 p.

Black, J. and Green, A. (1992). *Gods, Demons and Symbols of Ancient Mesopotamia*. British Museum Press. 192 p.

Blenkinsopp, J. (1985). The Documentary Hypothesis in trouble. *Bible Review* 1 (4), 22-32.

Bottero, J. (1987/92). *Mesopotamia: Writing, Reasoning, and the Gods*. Bahrani, Z. and van de Mieroop, M. (Trans.), Univ. Chicago Press. 311 p.

Braaten, L. J. (2001). The voice of Wisdom: a creation context for the emergence of Trinitarian language. *Wesleyan Theological J.* 36, 31-56.

Burney, C. (1977). *From Village to Empire/The Ancient Near East.* Phaidon/Univ. Cornell Press, 224 p.

Burstein, S. M. (1978). *The Babyloniaca of Berossus. Source and Monographs: Source from the Ancient Near East.* Undena Pubs., vol. 1, no. 5, 37 p.

Butzer, K. W. (1995). Environmental change in the Near East and human impact on the land. In: Sasson, J. M. (Ed.) *Civilizations of the Ancient Near East,* Simon & Schuster Macmillan, vol. 1, pp.123-151.

Campbell, S. (1992). The Halaf period in Iraq: old sites and new. *Biblical Archaeologist.* December, 1992

Clifford, R. J. (1972). *The Cosmic Mountain in Canaan and the Old Testament.* Harvard Univ. Press, 221 p.

Cooper, J. S. (1983). *The Curse of Agade.* Johns Hopkins Univ. Press, 292 p.

Dalley, S. (1989/1991). *Myths from Mesopotamia: Creation, The Flood, Gilgamesh, and Others.* Oxford Univ. Press, 337 p.

Dante Alighieri, In: Durling R. M. (Ed., 1996). *The divine comedy.* Oxford Univ. Press.

Englund, R. K. and Nissen, H. J. (1993). *Die lexikalischen Listen der Archaischen Texte aus Uruk.* Archaische Texte aus Uruk vol. **3,** Gebr. Mann Verlag. 319 p.

Fagan, B. M. (1979). *Return to Babylon: Travelers, Archaeologists, and Monuments in Mesopotamia.* Little, Brown & Co. 300 p.

Finegan, J. (1979). *Archaeological History of the Ancient Middle East.* Westview Press, 456 p.

Finkelstein, J. J. (1963). The antediluvian kings: a University of California tablet. *J. Cuneiform Studies* 17, 39-51.

Frankfort, H. (1933). Gods and myths on Sargonid seals. *Iraq* 1, 2-30.

Green, M. W. and Nissen, H. J. (1987). Zeichenliste der archaischen texte aus Uruk, *Archaische Texte aus Uruk Band 2.* Gebr. Mann Verlag,

Hallo, W. W. (1970). Antediluvian cities. *J. Cuneiform Studies* 23, 57-67.

Hallo, W. W. and Simpson, W. K. (1971/1998). *The Ancient Near East: A History.* Harcourt Brace College Pub., 324 p.

Heinrich, E. and Seidl, U. (1967). Grundrisszeichnungen aus dem alten Orient. *Mitteilungen der Deutschen Orient-Gesellschaft* 98, 24-45.

Howard-Carter, T. (1981). The tangible evidence for the earliest Dilmun. *J. Cuneiform Studies* 33, 210-223.

Jacobsen, T. (1939/1966). *The Sumerian King List. Assyriological Studies* 11, Univ. Chicago Press, 216 p.

Jacobsen, T. (1976). *The Treasures of Darkness: A History of Mesopotamian Religion.* Yale Univ. Press, 273 p.

Jacobsen, T. (1987). *The Harps That Once . . .* Yale Univ. Press, 498 p.

Johnson, M. D. (1969/1988). *The Purpose of the Biblical Genealogies.* Cambridge Univ. Press, 310 p.

Joyner, R. (1996). *The Final Quest.* Whitaker House Pub. 158 p.

King, L. W. (1902/1976). *Enuma Elish: The Seven Tablets of Creation,* Vols. 1 and 2. AMS Press (Reprint of original edition by Luzac and Co.), 274 p.

Kramer, S. N. (1944/1972). *Sumerian Mythology: A Study of Spiritual and Literary Achievement in the Third Millennium B. C.* Univ. Pennsylvania Press, 130 p.

Kramer, S. N. (1956/1981). *History Begins at Sumer.* Univ. Pennsylvania Press, 388 p.

Kramer, S. N. (1968). The Babel of tongues: a Sumerian version. *J. American Oriental Soc.* 88 (Speiser volume), 108-111.

Kramer, S. N. and Maier, J. (1989). *Myths of Enki, The Crafty God.* Oxford Univ. Press. 272 p.

Lamberg-Karlovsky, C. C. (1982). Dilmun: gateway to immortality. *J. Near Eastern Studies* 41, 45-50.

Lambert, W. G. (1992). Nippur in ancient ideology. In: deJong Ellis, M. (Ed.), *Nippur at the Centennial.* University Museum, Philadelphia, pp. 119-126.

Landmann, G., Reimer, A. and Kempe, S. (1996). Climatically induced lake level changes at Lake Van, Turkey, during the Pleistocene/Holocene transition. *Global Biogeochemical Cycles* 10, 797-808.

Larsen, M. T. (1994/1996). *The Conquest of Assyria: Excavations in an Antique Land, 1840-1860.* Routledge. 390 p.

Laurin, R. B. (1978). The tower of Babel revisited. In: Tuttle, G. A. (Ed.), *Biblical and Near Eastern Studies: Essays in Honor of William Sanford LaSor.* W.B. Erdmans, pp. 142-5.

Layard, A. H. (1849). *Nineveh and its Remains with an Account of a Visit to the Chaldean Christian of Kurdistan, and the Yezidis, or Devil Worshippers, and an Inquiry into the Manners and Arts of the Ancient Assyrians.*

Leick, G. (2001/2002). *Mesopotamia: The Invention of the City.* Penguin Books. 360 p.

Lloyd, S. (1947/1980). *Foundations in the Dust.* Thames and Hudson, 216 p.

Lloyd, S. (1978/1984). *The Archaeology of Mesopotamia: From the Old Stone Age to the Persian Conquest.* Thames and Hutton, 251 p.

Lyon, D. G. (1998). *Beginner's Assyrian.* Hippocrene Books Inc. 138 p.

Matthews, R. J. (1993). *Cities, Seals and Writing: Archaic Seal Impressions from Jamdet Nasr and Ur.* Gebr. Mann Verlag. 73 p.

Moorey, P. R. S. (1978). *Kish Excavations 1923–1933.* Oxford Univ. Press, 213 p.

Newman, J. P. (1876). *The Thrones and palaces of Babylon and Nineveh from sea to sea: a thousand miles on horseback.* Nelson and Phillips.

Nissen, H. J. (1983/1988).*The Early History of the Ancient Near East (9000 - 2000 B.C.).* Translated: Lutzeier, E. and Northcott, K. J. Univ. Chicago Press, 215 p.

Nissen, H. J., Damerow, P. and Englund, R. K. (1993). *Archaic Bookkeeping.* Univ. Chicago Press. 169 p.

Otto, R. (1923/1958), Harvey, J. W., Translator. *The Idea of the Holy.* Oxford Univ. Press, 232 p.

Postgate, J. N. (1992/1994). *Early Mesopotamia: Society and Economy at the Dawn of History.* Routledge, 367 p.

Pritchard, J. B. (1954). *Ancient Near Eastern Texts Relating to the Old Testament.* Princeton Univ. Press, 544 p.

Rawlinson, H. C. and Norris, E. (1861). *A Selection from the Historical Inscriptions of Chaldaea, Assyria, & Babylonia.* British Museum.

Rowton, M. B. (1960). The date of the Sumerian King List. *J. Near Eastern Studies* 19, 156-162.

Ryan, W. B. F. and Pitman, W. (1998). *Noah's Flood: The New Scientific Discoveries About the Event That Changed History.* Simon and Schuster. 317 p.

Ryan, W. B. F., Major, C. O., Lericolais, G. and Goldstein, S. L. (2003). Catastrophic flooding of the Black Sea. *Ann. Rev. Earth Planet. Sci.* 31, 525-554.

Saggs, H. W. F. (2000). *Peoples of the Past: Babylonians.* British Museum/Univ. Berkeley Press, 192 p.

Schmandt-Besserat, D. (1992). *Before Writing.* Univ. Texas Press.

Smith, G. (1876). *The Chaldean Account of Genesis (containing the description of the Creation, the Fall of Man, the Deluge, the Tower of Babel, the Times of the Patriarchs and Nimrod, Babylonian fables and legends of the gods from the cuneiform inscriptions).* Low, Marston, Searle, and Rivington. 319 p.

Sollberger, E. (1962). The Tummal Inscription. *J. Cuneiform Studies* 16, 40-47.

Van Buren, E. D. (1944). The Sacred Marriage in early times in Mesopotamia. Orientalia 13, 1-72.

Van Dijk, J. (1964-65). Le motif cosmique dans la pensee Sumerienne. *Acta Orientalia* 28, 1-59.

Wenham, G. J. (1978). The coherence of the flood narrative. *Vetus Testamentum* 28, 336-348.

Wenham, G. J. (1987). *Word Biblical Commentary, Volume 1: Genesis 1-15.* Word Books. 353 p.

Wilson, A. N. (1990). *C. S. Lewis: a Biography.* HarperCollins. 334 p.

Wilson, E. J. (1994). "Holiness" and "Purity" in Mesopotamia. *Alter Orient und Altes Testament*, Band 237, Verlag Butzon & Bercker Kevelaer, 121 p.

Wiseman, P. J. (1936/1977). *New discoveries in Babylonia about Genesis.* In: Wiseman, D. J. (Ed.), *Clues to Creation in Genesis*, Marshall, Morgan and Scott, 232 p.

Wiseman, P. J. (1948/1977). *Creation Revealed in Six Days.* In: Wiseman, D. J. (Ed.), *Clues to Creation in Genesis*, Marshall, Morgan and Scott, 232 p.

Woolley, C. L. (1936). *Abraham: Recent Discoveries and Hebrew Origins.* Faber and Faber Ltd. 299 p.

Woolley, C. L. (1939). *Ur Excavations, vol. 5: The Ziggurat and its Surroundings.* Trustees of the British and Pennsylvania Museums. 150 p.

Woolley, C. L. (1954/1963). *Excavations at Ur.* Ernest Benn Ltd. 256 p.

Index